TAKE the JOURNEY

34 Daily Devotions To Help You Go Against The Flow

LES CHRISTIE

COLLEGE PRESS PUBLISHING COMPANY • JOPLIN, MISSOURI

All Scripture quotations, unless indicated, are taken from
THE HOLY BIBLE: NEW INTERNATIONAL VERSION®.
Copyright © 1973, 1978, 1984 by International Bible Society.
Used by permission of Zondervan Publishing House.
All rights reserved.

International Standard Book Number 0-89900-714-7

DEDICATION

This book is fondly dedicated to my parents
Les and Margaret Christie
and my father- and mother-in-law
Burke and Mary Ellen Hintz.

ACKNOWLEDGMENTS

I am so appreciative for Jeff Mitchell, Jeromy Johnson, Bryan Allen, Kevin Batangan and especially Laurel Hall who made numerous contributions in selecting appropriate Scripture verses and thought-provoking questions for many of the devotions in this book.

I am so grateful for my faculty secretary, Amy Salter. She was able to take my handwritten scribbling and put it into a typed manuscript. She also offered some helpful insights into several of the devotions in the book. Her little Post-it® notes, stuck all over the original manuscript, were a lot of fun to read.

I am so thankful for College Press Publishing for their encouragement on this book. I am especially thankful for Chris DeWelt and John Hunter who were so very cordial, and enjoyable to work with.

I am also deeply indebted to my good friends at Christ In Youth. I have worked with them on a variety of projects for over twenty-five years. They have a tremendous staff including president Paul Smith, directors Dick Gibson, Andy Hansen, and Steve Sigler. I always look forward with great anticipation to visiting their offices and seeing Wade, Robin, Brenda, Tony, John, Kevin, Andy S., Kriss, Sharon, Dayla, Pat, Melia, Catherine, Genilyn, Lori, and Susan. I am grateful and feel very privileged that they will be featuring this book at their summer conferences and in their youth catalog of books.

TABLE OF CONTENTS

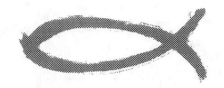

INTRODUCTION

HOW TO HAVE AN

EFFECTIVE QUIET TIME

Whether you call it quiet time, personal devotions, time of meditation, or your "appointment with God," this time is crucial for getting direction from God for your life, growing close to God and in your personal knowledge of God. It is more than just spending a few hurried minutes reading and praying. We need to meet with the Lord himself, to tell him of our deep love for him. When we bring our bruised selves to God, accept the truth that he knows our needs and how to heal us, and receive insights from his word for the day, then we have had true devotions.

Select a place to have your quiet time where you can be alone. If you have trouble concentrating, this may mean finding a room, park bench, or backyard where you will not be disturbed. If necessary it may mean mentally shutting out the world for a half an hour on a crowded schoolbus. Do whatever you have to do to find a place where you can concentrate and listen to God.

Select a time when you can be alert. First thing in the morning is a great time for many young people because it lets your quiet time set the tone for the day. However, if you are half asleep or frantic in the mornings but relaxed and alert in the evenings or right after school, do it then. Just be sure that unexpected demands don't crowd God out. Make a commitment with God for the next thirty some days that nothing will take priority over your daily meeting with him during the time you have set. Devotions are essential just as food is essential. Even food can be a bother at times, but we manage to eat regularly — some of us do a little munching on the side.

Select an amount of time you can be committed to every day of the week. Each devotion in this book is designed to take thirty minutes. Consistency, however, is the crucial element, even if you can manage only five to ten minutes a day in the beginning. If you only have a brief amount of time each day then go through different portions of each devotion, spending a few days on each devotion.

Commit yourself to go to bed at whatever time is necessary for you to be rested enough to be alert for God. If you have determined your quiet time with God takes priority over time spent with friends or television, then this will be possible.

There is not one way to have a quiet time. However, a little structure will help you avoid wasting time, while variety will keep you from getting bored.

One suggestion is to divide your time between the following six elements:
1. Pray
2. Read the illustration
3. Read the explanation (what's the point?)
4. Read the Scripture (meditating on God's word)
5. Work through the application (digging deeper)
6. Pray

Allow a large amount of time for application and prayer. Start your quiet time with prayer, asking God to enable you to understand what is written and to hear what he has to say to you. Be still for a moment before God. Ask God to cleanse your heart and guide your quiet time. Pray that you will thirst more for God and know him more fully. When you are finished going through steps two through five, praise God for what you read about him and talk to God about what application he can make evident for your own life. Ask him for grace to do what the passages command. Tell God about any sins you are struggling with, and ask for his power to abandon them. Thank God for special blessings.

Dedicate your day to the Lord, and pray over the details. Also listen for God's voice during your prayer time, but evaluate what you hear by the Bible. God won't ever contradict his written Word.

In the back of the book are places to write your prayer concerns or names of people you want to pray for. Many people find it helpful and encouraging to record their concerns and requests and then the date and answer God provides. There are additional pages to record your praises, thanking God for the blessings he has provided, many of them coming unexpectedly.

The devil will come up with dozens of excuses to keep you from meeting with God. Satan will convince you that you are too tired, you have some emergency to take care of, etc. He will keep you up so late at night that you have difficulty getting up for your quiet time if you let him. You must ask God daily for the strength to resist distractions, get enough rest, and keep your appointment with him.

Use your devotions all day. Ask God to saturate your mind with the things you have read and let them soak in as you go about your day. Implement them. Discuss them with a friend. Pass them along to another. You may even want to consider going through these devotions in a small group of two, three, four or five students.

I am hoping the next thirty some days you spend with God will make a difference in your life. I pray that God's peace will encompass you.

"The LORD bless you and keep you; the LORD make his face shine upon you and be gracious (kind, merciful, and giving favor) to you; the LORD turn his (approving) face toward you and give you peace (tranquility of heart and life continually)" Numbers 6:24-26 (words in parentheses from Amplified version). This beautiful blessing was devised by God himself at the first use of the tabernacle in the desert. He gave it to his own people — people like us.

Jesus referred to this same "peace" and expanded it when he said to his disciples in John 14:27, "Peace I leave with you; my peace I give you. I do not give to you as the world gives. Do not let your hearts be troubled and do not be afraid (stop allowing yourselves to be agitated and disturbed; and do not permit yourselves to be fearful and intimidated and cowardly, and unsettled)" (words in parentheses – Amplified).

"What does that fish stand for?"

This Christian symbol was created hundreds of years ago due to the threat of death when the church was under intense persecution. A believer would draw half of the fish in the dirt and another would complete the drawing to communicate their shared faith.

The fish is a very ancient symbol. An acronym was made using the Greek word "ichthus," meaning "fish." Each of the letters was regarded as the initial of a word in the sentence, "Iesous Christos, Theou Huios, Sopter," meaning "Jesus Christ, God's Son, Savior." Used in the first century, its meaning may not have been known to pagan persecutors, yet to early Christians it was an emblem of profound significance. It expressed the fact that we all need a Savior, and salvation comes through Jesus Christ.

I = Ἰησοῦς
X = Χριστὸς
Θ = Θεοῦ
Υ = Υἱὸς
Σ = Σωτήρ

I = Jesus
X = Christ
Θ = God's
Υ = Son
Σ = Savior

EXCELLENCE

ALBERTO SALAZAR
Marathon Runner

There are incredible stories of what an athlete will endure to achieve victory. In the 1982 Boston Marathon, Alberto Salazar ran the race of a lifetime. It was Monday, April 19, and Salazar was favored to win because he had already won five major events that year. He was the premier long-distance runner. He set a new world's record at the New York Marathon. As the gun sounded, it was 25-year-old Dick Beardsly who set the pace. Beardsly and Salazar strode along side by side, averaging an incredible 13 miles an hour as they raced down that roadway. They exchanged water bottles to keep their tongues from sticking to the roofs of their mouths. Every muscle in their body strained as they ran the entire marathon side by side. When it was over, Salazar had finished just two seconds ahead of Dick Beardsly. Salazar's face was milk white and stretched in agony as he collapsed past the finish line into the arms of two visiting policeman.

You don't realize what a marathon runner goes through until you watch them cross the finish line and continue to watch them for the next few moments. In a 1978 race, Salazar's temperature rose to 108 degrees and he actually received his last rites. On that day in Boston, a nurse went over to assist him and she put her hand under his arm and felt an unusual pulse. She took his temperature and discovered it was 88 degrees (hypothermia had set in). The incredible things he would endure! Later that day, Salazar's father admitted this to a newspaper reporter: "One of these days he is going to kill himself. He told me never in his life did he make an effort like he did today. He suffered more than ever before, but he never thought of quitting."

WHAT'S THE POINT?

Striving for excellence. Alberto Salazar wanted to be the best that he could be. The world wants us to be average. Politicians aim for the average person. Advertisers aim for the average person. Yet, when you get sick, you don't want an average doctor. When you need legal help, you don't want an average lawyer. When you are at war, you don't want an average general to lead you. In your spiritual walk, don't be a pew potato. Strive to do and be your best.

MEDITATING ON GOD'S WORD

2 Chronicles 31:21
"...he...worked wholeheartedly. And so he prospered."

Ecclesiastes 9:10
"Whatever your hand finds to do, do it with all your might."

1 Corinthians 12:31
We are to walk in a more excellent way.

Colossians 3:23
"Whatever you do, work at it with all of your heart, as working for the Lord, not for men."

Hebrews 1:4
Jesus has been given a more excellent name.

Hebrews 8:6
Jesus has a more excellent ministry.

DIGGING DEEPER

1. What do you enjoy doing most? What do you enjoy doing least? Why?

2. What if you could re-do one thing you did half-heartedly in your past? What would you choose? How can you guard against this happening again in the future?

3. How can doing your best at whatever you do be a positive influence on others?

4. What would cause a human being to endure that kind of physical pain and strain?

5. What was the last project/activity you worked on with all your might? Why was the project/activity so important to you?

6. How does Colossians 3:23 apply to your school and your part time job if you are working?

7. What people/things are hindering you from striving for excellence in your own life? What can you do to change the situation?

8. What do you need to do to walk in a more excellent way?

RELIABILITY

ALEXANDER THE GREAT
Military General

Alexander the Great, one of the greatest military generals who ever lived, conquered almost the entire known world with his vast army. One night during a campaign, he couldn't sleep and left his tent to walk around the campgrounds.

As he was walking he came across a soldier asleep on guard duty — a serious offense. The penalty for falling asleep on guard duty was, in some cases, instant death; the commanding officer sometimes poured kerosene on the sleeping soldier and lit it.

The soldier began to wake up as Alexander the Great approached him. Recognizing who was standing in front of him, the young man feared for his life.

"Do you know what the penalty is for falling asleep on guard duty?" Alexander the Great asked the soldier.

"Yes, sir," the soldier responded in a quivering voice.

"Soldier, what's your name?" demanded Alexander the Great.

"Alexander, sir."

Alexander the Great repeated the question: "What is your name?"

"My name is Alexander, sir," the soldier repeated.

A third time and more loudly Alexander the Great asked, "What is your name?"

A third time the soldier meekly said, "My name is Alexander, sir."

Alexander the Great then looked the young soldier straight in the eye. "Soldier," he said with intensity, "either change your name or change your conduct."

(From *Hot Illustrations for Youth*, by Wayne Rice. Copyright 1994 by Youth Specialties. Used by permission.)

WHAT'S THE POINT?

We who carry the name of Christ and call ourselves Christian must live our lives in a Christlike manner.

MEDITATING ON GOD'S WORD

Ephesians 1:4
"For he chose us in him before the creation of the world to be holy and blameless in his sight."

Colossians 3:12
"Therefore, as God's chosen people, holy and dearly loved, clothe yourselves with compassion, kindness, humility, gentleness, and patience."

2 Timothy 2:19
"'The Lord knows those who are his,' and 'Everyone who confesses the name of the Lord must turn away from wickedness.'"

James 2:7
"Are they not the ones who are slandering the noble name of him to whom you belong?"

Revelation 3:8
"I know your deeds. See, I have placed before you an open door that no one can shut. I know that you have little strength, yet you have kept my word and have not denied my name."

DIGGING DEEPER

1. Do you know what your name means? What? How does that make you feel?

2. Do your friends know you are a Christian? How do they know?

3. Have you ever denied being a Christian? When? Why?

4. What are things a Christian should pursue? What are things a Christian should flee from?

5. What specific things do you need to turn away from?

6. How is it comforting to realize God knows we have little strength on our own?

PRIORITIES

SWITCHING PRICE TAGS

Some pranksters broke into a sporting goods store in San Francisco several years ago. Instead of robbing the store, they simply switched all the price tags.

The next morning when the store opened people began bringing up all kinds of oddly priced items to the checkout cashier. Tennis rackets were selling for $1 and white socks had price tags of $485. It was a mess and they had to close the store for two days.

(From *Hot Illustrations for Youth*, by Wayne Rice. Copyright 1994 by Youth Specialties. Used by permission.)

WHAT'S THE POINT?

When I came to Jesus, he changed all the price tags in my life. Things that I had thought were so important were no longer important at all. Things that I thought had no value or were a low priority were now extremely valuable and high on my list of priorities. My values were changed when I came to Christ.

MEDITATING ON GOD'S WORD

Matthew 6:24-33
"No one can serve two masters. Either he will hate the one and love the other, or he will be devoted to the one and despise the other. You cannot serve both God and Money. Therefore I tell you,

do not worry about your life, what you will eat or drink; or about your body, what you will wear. Is not life more important than food, and the body more important than clothes? Look at the birds of the air; they do not sow or reap or store away in barns, and yet your heavenly Father feeds them. Are you not much more valuable than they? Who of you by worrying can add a single hour to his life? And why do you worry about clothes? See how the lilies of the field grow. They do not labor or spin. Yet I tell you that not even Solomon in all his splendor was dressed like one of these. If that is how God clothes the grass of the field, which is here today and tomorrow is thrown into the fire, will he not much more clothe you, O you of little faith? So do not worry, saying, 'What shall we eat?' or 'What shall we drink?' or 'What shall we wear?' For the pagans run after all these things, and your heavenly Father knows that you need them. But seek first his kingdom and his righteousness, and these things will be given to you as well."

Acts 13:9
"Then Saul, who was also called Paul..."

Romans 6:4
"We were therefore buried with him through baptism into death in order that, just as Christ was raised from the dead through the glory of the Father, we too may live a new life."

DIGGING DEEPER

1. Who were the three most important people in your life before you became a Christian? What about now?

2. If your house caught on fire, what five things would you rescue besides people and pets? Why?

3. How have your priorities changed since you have accepted Christ? Why?

4. The Apostle Paul changed so dramatically that he changed his name from Saul to Paul. What changes have occurred in your life since becoming a Christian?

5. What further changes do you need to make in your life now that you are a Christian?

6. Do you honestly believe God will take care of the necessities in your life? Why do we still concern ourselves with these things?

7. Do you find yourself at times torn between trusting God and trusting in your own abilities? How does the passage in Matthew apply to you?

4

FAITH

BLONDIN
Tightrope Walker

In the 1860's there was a famous tightrope walker named Blondin. He toured the entire country putting on exhibitions. He went to Niagara Falls to put on a three-day show. Blondin stretched the tightrope across the falls and for two days he walked this rope, drawing a tremendous crowd. On the third day he said he was going to walk the rope blindfolded and pushing a wheelbarrow. Before he tried this feat he went around among the crowd and asked "Do you believe I can do this?" There wasn't one in the crowd who doubted. So he climbed up on the rope and asked, "If you really think I can do it who will come up and get in the wheelbarrow?"

(From *Hot Illustrations for Youth*, by Wayne Rice. Copyright 1994 by Youth Specialties. Used by permission.)

WHAT'S THE POINT?

People believe in Jesus like they believe in George Washington, Abraham Lincoln, or Napoleon. Biblically, belief means "trusting oneself to." It means trusting and believing enough to get in the wheelbarrow. It means trusting Jesus with your life.

MEDITATING ON GOD'S WORD

Psalm 62:8
"Trust in him at all times, O people; pour out your hearts to him, for God is our refuge."

Matthew 6:25, 30
"Therefore...do not worry about your life, what you will eat or drink...O you of little faith."

Romans 5:1 (Living)
"So now, since we have been made right in God's sight by faith in his promises, we can have real peace with him because of what Jesus Christ our Lord has done for us."

Galatians 3:11
"Clearly no one is justified before God by the law, because 'The righteous will live by faith.'"

Ephesians 2:8-9
"For it is by grace you have been saved, through faith — and this is not from yourselves, it is the gift of God — not by works, so that no one can boast."

James 2:14-18
"What good is it, my brothers, if a man claims to have faith but has no deeds? Can such faith save him? Suppose a brother or sister is without clothes and daily food. If one of you says to him, 'Go, I wish you well; keep warm and well fed,' but does nothing about his physical needs, what good is it? In the same way, faith by itself, if it is not accompanied by action, is dead. But someone will say, 'You have faith; I have deeds.' Show me your faith without deeds, and I will show you my faith by what I do."

DIGGING DEEPER

1. As a child, in whom did you have the greatest faith?

2. What are some ordinary things you put your trust/faith in? (example: flying in an airplane)

3. Where are you in the crowd at Niagara Falls?
   A. Way in the back where no one can see you
   B. Somewhere in the middle, trying to blend in with everyone else
   C. In front, looking for someone else to volunteer
   D. Getting into the wheelbarrow

4. What causes you the greatest amount of worry? What would God need to do to get rid of your worries?

5. Why do you think God chose grace rather than works?

6. Which comes first, "faith" or "deeds"? Why?

7. What good works has God created you for?

8. How do the verses in James compare with Galatians 3:1-14?

9. Where in your life are you most in need of faith?

10. How did these people put their faith in the Lord?
    Noah (Genesis 6:14-22)
    Abraham (Genesis 22:1-10)
    Joseph (Genesis 50:20)
    David (1 Samuel 17:36-47)
    Daniel (Daniel 6)

STEADFASTNESS

ERIC LIDDELL

Olympic Runner

For months, Eric Liddell trained as a track athlete for the purpose of winning the 100 meter race in the Olympics of 1924. Sportswriters all over the world predicted he would win the 100 meters.

Then he learned that the 100 meter race in the Olympics of 1924 would be run on Sunday. It posed a problem. Eric believed, right or wrong, that he could not honor God by running in the contest on the Lord's day.

His fans were stunned by his refusal to run. Some who had praised him the week before began to call him a fool. The press laughed at him because he wouldn't run on a Sunday.

A couple of days later, a runner dropped out of the 400 meter race and Eric offered to take the spot, even though it was four times the race he had trained to run.

Eric won the race. God gave him his gold medal. God honored his reverence for the Lord.

WHAT'S THE POINT?

Eric took a stand and it cost him a gold medal in the 100 meters. He had his values straight in his mind. He knew what was important in his life over the long haul. His commitment to the Lord was paramount in his life. The Lord came first, no matter what the price. He would not be swayed by the whims of the crowd.

MEDITATING ON GOD'S WORD

Joshua 1:7
"Be strong and very courageous…"

1 Kings 11:4
"As Solomon grew old, his wives turned his heart after other gods, and his heart was not fully devoted to the LORD his God…"

Psalm 57:7
"My heart is steadfast, O God…."

Daniel 1:8 (Living)
"But Daniel made up his mind that he would not eat the food given to him by the King."

1 Corinthians 15:58
"Therefore, my dear brothers, stand firm. Let nothing move you."

Galatians 6:9
"Let us not become weary in doing good, for at the proper time we will reap a harvest if we do not give up."

Philippians 4:1
"Therefore, my brothers, you whom I love and long for, my joy and crown, that is how you should stand firm in the Lord, dear friends!"

DIGGING DEEPER

1. Do you have beliefs (you hold them) and convictions (they hold you)? Have you ever compromised a belief or conviction you had in order to avoid conflict or criticism? Why?

2. What would you have done if you were in Eric Liddell's place? Was he being overzealous in his beliefs? Why? How do you think the Lord felt about his decision?

3. In what areas of your life do you need encouragement and strength?

4. When in your life have you felt the most free? Why?

5. How will you seek to please God this week?

6

ENDURANCE

CHARIOTS OF FIRE

In the movie *Chariots of Fire* (you can rent it on video), there is a key moment I have not forgotten. I can see it in my mind as if it were yesterday. Eric Liddell is in a race in Scotland. As he and the other runners are going into a turn, one of his fellow runners elbows him. He loses his balance and trips into the infield.

As the other runners continue on, Eric Liddell, for an instant, lies upon the infield watching them, daring to think that the race has been lost. You watch Eric Liddell lying there on the grass and you wonder what he will do. Suddenly, he gets up and with even greater vigor than before, he starts to catch up and he eventually wins the race.

Those who knew Eric Liddell say that it is a true story and actually happened.

WHAT'S THE POINT?

2 Samuel 16:14 says "And the king and all the people with him, arrived weary at the Jordan, and there he refreshed himself." I wonder to myself, "What was in the heart of Eric Liddell that caused him to not quit, but in the moment of *his* Jordan caused him to get up and run again?" I'm convinced that it was something drilled into his heart and competitive spirit long before the gun of that race ever sounded. I'm positive that there are many of you who are in Eric Liddell's position on the infield

grass. You have been blasted for one reason or another, and you're tired and at your Jordan. The question for you is, "Are you going to get up, refresh yourself at the Lord's table, and run again?"

MEDITATING ON GOD'S WORD

Psalms 37:24
"Though he stumble, he will not fall, for the LORD upholds him with his hand."

Matthew 24:13
"But he who stands firm to the end will be saved."

John 8:31
"If you hold to my teaching, you are really my disciples."

1 Corinthians 15:58
"Therefore, my brothers, stand firm. Let nothing move you. Always give yourself fully to the work of the Lord, because you know that your labor is not in vain."

Galatians 6:9
"Let us not become weary in doing good, for at a proper time, we will reap a harvest if we do not give up."

2 Timothy 4:5 (Living)
"Stand steady, and don't be afraid of suffering for the Lord. Bring others to Christ. Leave nothing undone that you ought to do."

Hebrews 12:1-2
"Therefore, since we are surrounded by such a great cloud of witnesses, let us throw off everything that hinders and the sin that so easily entangles, and let us run with perseverance the race marked out for us. Let us fix our eyes on Jesus, the author and perfecter of our faith, who for the joy set before him endured the cross, scorning its shame, and sat down at the right hand of the throne of God."

DIGGING DEEPER

1. What is the hardest thing you have ever had to endure?

2. How did you get through that time?

3. How has that experience helped shape you into who you are today?

4. What was the key element that helped you through your hardship?

5. You've been running a good race, but you trip and fall into the infield.
   What are you going to do?
   A. Give up
   B. Get up and walk it off
   C. Jog the rest of the way
   D. Get up and run the rest of the race as best you can

6. Is your life more like a
   A. sprinter
   B. marathon runner
   C. high hurdler
   WHY?

7. How have you been persecuted for your faith?

8. What are the three actions (each introduced by "let us") that Christians are commanded to do as they run the race according to Hebrews?

9. What does it mean to throw off everything that hinders us?

10. What comfort do you get from knowing that a cloud of witnesses is watching you run the Christian race?

11. What are two obstacles that hinder and entangle your race? What are you going to do about them?

12. What is the hardest thing you are going through right now?

ADDICTION

FISHING EAGLES

National Geographic aired a special one night about how eagles catch fish in lakes. They fly high above the water but their eyesight is so good they can spot fish in the water below. When they see one they fold back their wings and aim directly for the water, going as fast as 130 mph. When they reach the water they spread their wings, reach out their talons, grab the fish, and begin flying back to the shore.

On this TV special, they showed film of a very unusual occurrence. An eagle made a dive for a fish and grabbed it in its talons. But the fish was much larger than the eagle realized. As it began to fly to the shore you could see the strain on the eagle's face. It was not going to make it to the shore with this huge fish. It then tried to drop the fish, to let go of it. But the talons of the eagle had dug into the flesh of the fish so deeply that it could not pull them out. It struggled but to no avail.

Slowly the eagle descended into the lake and drowned, unable to let loose of its catch.

(From *More Hot Illustrations for Youth*, by Wayne Rice. Copyright 1995 by Youth Specialties. Used by permission.)

WHAT'S THE POINT?

Many times in life we grab on to something that can be dangerous. We feel we have control and can stop holding on any time we like. It becomes a habit and one day we try to get out and discover that we no longer have a hold of it but it has a hold of us.

MEDITATING ON GOD'S WORD

Proverbs 4:14-15
"Do not set foot on the path of the wicked or walk in the way of evil men. Avoid it, do not travel on it; turn from it and go on your way."

Proverbs 6:27
"Can a man scoop fire into his lap without his clothes being burned?"

Matthew 26:41
"Watch and pray so that you will not fall into temptation."

Romans 12:1-2
"Therefore, I urge you...do not conform any longer to the pattern of this world, but be transformed by the renewing of your mind."

Romans 12:21
"Do not be overcome by evil, but overcome evil with good."

1 Corinthians 9:2
"No, I beat my body and make it my slave so that after I have preached to others, I myself will not be disqualified for the prize."

1 Corinthians 10:13
"No temptation has seized you except what is common to man. And God is faithful; he will not let you be tempted beyond what you can bear. But when you are tempted, he will also provide a way out so that you can stand up under it."

2 Timothy 2:22
"Flee the evil desires of youth, and pursue righteousness, faith, love, and peace."

Hebrews 4:15
"For we do not have a high priest who is unable to sympathize with our weaknesses, but we have one who has been tempted in every way, just as we are — yet was without sin."

Hebrews 12:1

"Therefore, since we are surrounded by such a great cloud of witnesses, let us throw off everything that hinders and the sin that so easily entangles, and let us run with perseverance the race marked out for us."

DIGGING DEEPER

1. Is there anything in your life that seems to be pulling you down? How?

2. Have you told anyone about it? If not, who would you trust telling about your situation?

3. In what ways do you tend to conform to the world?

4. What are some of the world's major influences on your life?

5. How have you tried to break away from worldly influences?

6. What does it mean that Jesus was without sin? Why then, should we approach him with confidence?

7. Can you think of times in your life where you have been tempted and God has given you a way of escape? Did you take the way of escape or did you do the sin anyway? How did you feel?

PURITY

ELIMINATING DARKNESS

Wouldn't it be silly for me to go into a darkened room and try to get rid of the darkness in the room by trying to collect the darkness in a trash bag? Can you imagine attempting to gather the darkness into a trash bag. I'd try to clear out all the darkness, then I would turn on the light switch and let the light come into the room. You can't do that. It not only looks ridiculous, it can't be done.

Everybody knows you turn the light on and the light gets rid of the darkness in a room. The light eliminates the darkness.

WHAT'S THE POINT?

Many of us are trying to clean up our own lives; we are trying to get rid of the darkness. When we get our lives together and cleaned up, then we will come to Jesus. The problem is none of us can clean up our own lives. We need to let Jesus into our lives and he will get rid of the darkness. When we try to do it on our own, we look as silly as trying to put darkness in a room into a trash bag.

MEDITATING ON GOD'S WORD

Psalms 51:7
"Cleanse me with hyssop, and I will be clean; wash me and I will be whiter than snow."

Proverbs 20:9
"Who can say, 'I have kept my heart pure. I am without sin'?"

Proverbs 30:12
"Those who are pure in their own eyes yet are not cleansed of their filth."

Isaiah 1:18
"Though your sins are like scarlet, they shall be as white as snow."

Isaiah 6:6-7
"Then one of the seraphs flew to me with a live coal in his hand, which he had taken with tongs from the altar. With it he touched my mouth and said, 'See, this has touched your lips; your guilt is taken away and your sin atoned for.'"

Romans 3:22-24
"This righteousness from God comes through faith in Jesus Christ to all who believe. There is no difference, for all have sinned and fall short of the glory of God, and are justified freely by his grace through the redemption that came by Christ Jesus."

Romans 5:6-8
"You see, at just the right time, when we were still powerless, Christ died for the ungodly. Very rarely will anyone die for a righteous man, though for a good man someone might possibly dare to die. But God demonstrates his own love for us in this: While we were still sinners, Christ died for us."

James 4:8
"Come near to God and he will come near to you. Wash your hands, you sinners, and purify your hearts, you double-minded."

DIGGING DEEPER

1. Why is it impossible to be friends with both the world and with God?

2. Have you been guilty of two-timing God?

3. Is there something in your life that you don't want God to control? Are you waiting to get it under your control before you let God have it?

4. Are you afraid that God will love you less if he finds out you're not perfect? Do you really think he doesn't already know the imperfection in your life?

5. When did you first become aware of your sinfulness and your need for God?

6. What motivated you to turn to God?

7. If you had to explain the gospel message from these passages, what would you say?

8. How do you keep from being overpowered by the world's value structure?

COURAGE

LIGHTING THE FIRST CANDLE

Several years ago in Timisoara, Romania, Laszlo Tokes became pastor of Timisoara's small Hungarian Reformed Church. Tokes preached the gospel boldly, and within two years membership had swelled to five thousand.

But success can be dangerous in a Communist country. Authorities stationed police officers in front of the church on Sundays, cradling machine guns. They hired thugs to attack Pastor Tokes. They confiscated his ration book so he couldn't buy food or fuel. Finally, in December 1989, they decided to send him into exile.

But when police arrived to hustle Pastor Tokes away, they were stopped cold. Around the entrance of the church stood a wall of humanity. Members of other churches — Baptist, Adventist, Pentecostal, Orthodox, Catholic — had joined together to protest.

Though police tried to disperse the crowd, the people held their post all day and into the night. Then, just after midnight, a 19-year-old Baptist student named Daniel Gavra pulled out a packet of candles. He lit one and passed it to his neighbor.

When Tokes peered out the window, he was struck by the warm glow reflecting off hundreds of faces. That moment, he said later, was the "turning point in my life." His religious prejudices evaporated. Here were members of the body of Christ, completely disregarding denominational divisions, joining hands in his defense.

It was a moving testimony to Christian unity.

The crowd stayed all through the night — and the next night. Finally police broke through. They bashed in the church door, bloodied Pastor Tokes' face, then paraded him and his wife through the crowd and out into the night.

But that was not the end.

No, the religious protest led — as it always does — to political protest. The people streamed to the city square and began a full-scale demonstration against the Communist government. Again Daniel passed out his candles.

First they had burned for Christian unity; now they burned for freedom.

This was more than the government could tolerate. They brought in troops and ordered them to open fire on the crowd. Hundreds were shot. Young Daniel felt a searing pain as his leg was blown off. But the people of Timisoara stood bravely against the barrage of bullets.

And by their example they inspired the entire population of Romania. Within days the nation had risen up and the bloody dictator Ceausescu was gone.

For the first time in half a century, Romanians celebrated Christmas in freedom.

Daniel celebrated in the hospital, where he was learning to walk with crutches. His pastor came to offer sympathy, but Daniel wasn't looking for sympathy.

"Pastor, I don't mind so much the loss of a leg," he said. " After all, it was I who lit the first candle."

The candle that lit up an entire country.

(From *More Hot Illustrations for Youth,* by Wayne Rice. Copyright 1995 by Youth Specialties. Used by permission.)

WHAT'S THE POINT?

With a candle, a nineteen-year-old boy sparked a revolution that is still being felt today. Romania is a free country thanks to the efforts of people like Daniel Gavra who were willing to put their lives on the line for the sake of the gospel and for basic human rights.

You can make a difference wherever you are if you are willing to take a stand. Don't wait for everyone else to do it. Be the first to light your candle.

MEDITATING ON GOD'S WORD

Deuteronomy 31:6
"Be strong and courageous. Do not be afraid or terrified because of them, for the LORD your God goes with you; he will never leave you nor forsake you."

Joshua 1:9
"Have I not commanded you? Be strong and courageous. Do not be terrified; do not be discouraged, for the LORD your God will be with you wherever you go."

Proverbs 28:1
"The wicked man flees though no one pursues, but the righteous are as bold as a lion."

1 Corinthians 15:58
"Therefore, my dear brothers, stand firm. Let nothing move you. Always give yourselves fully to the work of the Lord, because you know that your labor in the Lord is not in vain."

1 Corinthians 16:13
"Be on your guard; stand firm in the faith; be men of courage; be strong."

Ephesians 6:10
"Finally, be strong in the Lord and in his mighty power."

Philippians 1:27-28
"...I will know that you stand firm in one spirit, contending as

one man for the faith of the gospel without being frightened in any way by those who oppose you."

2 Timothy 1:7
"For God did not give us a spirit of timidity, but a spirit of power, of love and of self-discipline."

DIGGING DEEPER

1. What one word describes your life?

2. How would you define courage?

3. What has been the greatest adventure you have ever had? What happened? Who was with you?

4. What was the last heroic thing you did?

5. When was the last time you took a stand for Christ?

6. When have you felt the strongest in your spiritual walk?

7. When was the last time you were attacked in spiritual battle? What happened?

8. Where is the battlefield in your life now?

9. What situation in your life requires a great deal of courage, of strength? How can others help you face this situation?

10. What was the toughest situation you had this week? Why was it so difficult? How did you deal with it? What good, if any came out of it?

11. When you hear that God has given you not a spirit of timidity, but of power, of love, and of self-discipline, how do you feel? If you believed this more, how would your life change? Why?

10

GOD'S LOVE

ATLAS

Lay Down Your Burden

Remember Atlas from Greek mythology? He led the Titans in their contest with Zeus and his punishment was being condemned to stand forever supporting the earth and heaven on his head, hands, and shoulders. The myth said if he moved, the earth would shake. He had the weight of the whole world on his back.

As I speak around the country I meet young people all the time who are mistakenly carrying the burden of earning God's love. Just watching their lifestyle is depressing. I want to say to Atlas, "Hey, Atlas, drop the globe and dance on it!" I want to say to students, "Let God embrace you with his love."

You can't buy God's love, you can't earn it or win it, and you don't deserve it. You just receive it. Jesus says "Come, you weary Christian Atlases and lay down your burden. I will comfort you." The extravagant love of God can be very disturbing.

WHAT'S THE POINT?

Love is searched for by every person on this earth. Most people find emptiness and loneliness. God loves us not because we are worthy, but because of who he is. The fact that God's love is based on nothing we do should make us feel very secure. Instead of running away from God, as many students who have never met him do, we should be running into his wide open loving arms. We need to crawl up on his lap and let him hold us close to his chest and rock us to sleep.

MEDITATING ON GOD'S WORD

Psalm 139:13-14
"For you created my inmost being; you knit me together in my mother's womb. I praise you because I am fearfully and wonderfully made; your works are wonderful. I know that full well."

Jeremiah 31:3
"I have loved you with an everlasting love."

Galatians 2:20-21
"...The life I live in the body, I live by faith in the Son of God, who loved me and gave himself for me. I do not set aside the grace of God, for if righteousness could be gained through the law, Christ died for nothing!"

Ephesians 2:4
"Because of his great love for us...."

Philippians 4:19
"And my God will meet all your needs according to his glorious riches in Christ Jesus."

1 Peter 5:7
"Cast all your anxiety on him because he cares for you."

1 John 3:1
"How great is the love the Father has lavished on us, that we should be called children of God."

1 John 4:19
"We love because he first loved us."

DIGGING DEEPER

1. What does God's love mean to you?

2. How would you finish this sentence: "Love is like...."

3. How have you experienced God's lavish love this week?

4. When did you come to accept the fact that God loved you no matter how bad you'd been? How did this understanding change you?

5. Are you doing things to please God to make him love you more? Is it possible for God to love you more than he does right now?

6. Do you sometimes doubt God's gift of salvation because it is too easy?

7. What is the source of human love? How can God's love be expressed through humans?

8. What has helped you to love others? What has inhibited your ability to love?

9. How has God's love helped you deal with your fears?

10. How has life changed since you met Christ?

11. Who do you know that is in need of God's love? What actions will you take today to communicate that love to them?

POTENTIAL

FRITZ KREISLER
Violinist

The story is told of a wealthy Englishman who had a collection of rare violins. There was one instrument that was of such quality and magnificence that the eminent violinist Fritz Kreisler desired to have it from this wealthy Englishman, but the owner did not want to sell it.

One day Kreisler came to see him. He could play with such virtuosity, perhaps unequaled, that he begged the man to let him play this marvelous instrument. The request was granted and the great violinist picked up the violin and played it as only Fritz Kreisler could play it. He forgot himself and poured his soul into the music. As the master artist played, the Englishman stood as one enchanted.

When Kreisler finished, not a word was spoken. He loosened the bow and strings, and placed the instrument in its case with the gentleness of a mother putting a baby in its bed. The owner then exclaimed, "Mr. Kreisler, you cannot buy the violin; take the violin. I have no right to keep it; it ought to belong to one who can make such beautiful music with it."

WHAT'S THE POINT?

God can make beautiful music with your life. But you have got to give him your life!

Exodus 32:29
"Then Moses said, 'You have been set apart for service to the LORD today…and he has blessed you this day.'"

1 Samuel 16:7
"…The LORD does not look at the things man looks at. Man looks at the outward appearance, but the LORD looks at the heart."

Jeremiah 32:17
"Nothing is too hard for you."

John 12:36
"Put your trust in the light while you have it, so that you may become sons of light."

1 Corinthians 2:9
No one has ever seen this, and no one has ever heard about it. No one has ever imagined what God has prepared for those who love him.

2 Corinthians 4:16
"Therefore we do not lose heart. Though outwardly we are wasting away, yet inwardly we are being renewed day by day."

Ephesians 5:8
In the past, you were full of darkness, but now you are full of light in the Lord. So live like children who belong to the light.

Philippians 1:6
"Being confident of this, that he who began a good work in you will carry it on to completion until the day of Christ Jesus."

Philippians 2:13
"For it is God who works in you to will and to act according to his good purposes."

Philippians 4:13
"I can do everything through him who gives me strength."

1 Peter 3:4
Your beauty should come from within you — the beauty of a gentle and quiet spirit that will never be destroyed and is very precious before God.

DIGGING DEEPER

1. If you were going to describe your life in terms of garden tools, what tool would you choose? Why?

2. How afraid of the dark were you as a child?

3. In what sense is darkness a good description of a life controlled by sin?

4. How have your thoughts, actions, and attitudes changed as a result of being touched by Christ?

5. In John 2:1-11, Jesus turned water into wine. In what area of your life do you need Jesus to turn water into wine? (for example: family, self-esteem, work, appearance, spiritual life, mental focus)

6. When in your life has the wine run out? How has Jesus replenished you?

7. What evidences have you had this week of God working in your life?

8. How can your Christian friends help you on your Christian pilgrimage?

ASSURANCE

IT IS WELL WITH MY SOUL

At the time it sailed away from New York in November 1873, the French liner, S.S. Ville du Havre, was the most luxurious ship afloat. Among her passengers was Mrs. H.G. Spafford of Chicago, making the trip with her four children: Maggie, Tanetta, Annie, and Bessie. Mr. Spafford was unable to make the voyage with his family because of business commitments in Chicago, so recently ravaged by the Great Fire. But, even though he was happy that his family was traveling on a ship with Christian companions, some last-minute premonition made him change the cabin they occupied to one toward the bow of the vessel. He told them, "Goodbye," promising to meet them in France in a few weeks.

At two o'clock on the morning of November 22, 1873, when the luxury liner was several days out and sailing on a quiet sea, she was rammed by the English iron sailing vessel, the Lochearn. In two hours, the Ville du Havre, one of the largest ships afloat, settled to the bottom of the ocean, with a loss of some two hundred and twenty-six lives, including the four Spafford children. Nine days later when the survivors landed at Cardiff, Wales, Mrs. Spafford cabled her husband these two words, "Saved alone." For him it was a second time of testing, coming almost too soon upon the heels of the first. In the Chicago Fire, he had lost everything he owned; in the tragedy at sea, he had lost his four precious children. As soon as he could, he booked passage on a ship to Europe to join his wife. On the way over, in December of that same year, 1873, the captain called him into his cabin and said, "I believe we are now passing over the place where the Ville du Havre went down."

That night he found it hard to sleep. But faith soon conquered doubt and there, in the mid-Atlantic, out of his heartbreak and pain, Mr. Spafford wrote five stanzas, the first of which contained these lines:

> When peace like a river attendeth my way,
> When sorrows like sea-billows roll,
> Whatever my lot, Thou hast taught me to say,
> "It is well, it is well with my soul!"

WHAT'S THE POINT?

Assurance: something you can count on, something you can trust. When life is treating us well or when life throws us in a well of despair, Jesus is still holding us, assuring us of our safety in him. Whatever life may throw our way, God is there to help see us through. You can count on it!

MEDITATING ON GOD'S WORD

Psalms 23:4
"Even though I walk through the valley of the shadow of death, I will fear no evil, for you are with me...."

Psalm 46:1-3 (Max Lucado Inspirational Study Bible)
"God is our protection and our strength. He always helps us in times of trouble. So we will not be afraid even if the earth shakes, or if the mountain falls into the sea, or if the oceans roar and foam..."

Nahum 1:7
"The LORD is good, a refuge in times of trouble. He cares for those who trust in him."

Romans 8:38-39 (Max Lucado Inspirational Study Bible)
"Yes, I am sure that neither death, nor life, nor angels, nor ruling spirits, nothing now, nothing in the future, no powers, nothing above us, nothing below us, nor anything else in the whole world

will ever be able to separate us from the love of God that is in Jesus Christ our Lord."

2 Thessalonians 2:16-17 (Max Lucado Inspirational Study Bible)
"May our Lord Jesus Christ himself and God our Father encourage you and strengthen you in every good thing you do and say. God loved us, and through his grace he gave us a good hope and encouragement that continues forever."

1 Peter 5:7
"Cast all your anxiety on him because he cares for you."

DIGGING DEEPER

1. Describe how you would envision Mr. Spafford's reaction the moment he first received the cable. How would you react?

2. How would you describe the place your life is at now: joyful or sorrowful? Why?

3. How is God allowing you to go through the school of hard knocks now? Can you see God at work through it?

4. How can you experience the peace and assurance that the Lord gives?

5. What confidence can Christians have about the events in their life? Why?

6. Have you ever felt separated from God's love? What was the reason? How do you feel after reading Romans 8?

TRUST

BALLOON MAN

There was a man who carried brightly colored balloons with him everywhere he went. He enjoyed watching them float above his head. And it was easy to hold the string in his hand or wrap it around his wrist and take his colorful balloons wherever he went. The other people where he worked were accustomed to seeing them. They didn't mind; it brightened the office a little. Even at night the balloons would float above the man as he slept.

One day he went to the fair and had a great time. At the fair he could blend into the atmosphere of the rides and lights and noise. Oh, sometimes people tried to buy his balloons, thinking he was a vendor, but of course he wouldn't sell even one.

At one of the booths he filled in a ticket to see if he could win a free ocean cruise. He certainly didn't plan on winning, but it wouldn't hurt to try. Yet two weeks later a telegram came — he had won! He would enjoy great entertainment and the world's finest chef providing his meals. Talk about excited! The man started packing immediately. He was ready to go days before it was time to leave.

On the morning of the big day, he called a taxi and had the driver take him to the dock very slowly because the balloons wouldn't all fit in the taxi and he had to hold some of them out the window. At the dock he unloaded his luggage, went aboard ship, and was welcomed by the officials who had planned his trip. They even had someone take his suitcases down to his cabin while he stayed on deck and enjoyed the activity. The ship was crowded. Many people were aboard just to say goodbye to friends. Confetti, horns, streamers — and lots of balloons. He felt right at home.

Eventually the visitors left and the voyage was begun. It was great! Sailing on a big ocean liner was really refreshing. It also made him very hungry. Someone told the balloon man that the evening meal was in just one hour — a welcome relief!

When they rang the bell, he started to walk toward the dining room on the second deck. The aroma of the food was so enticing. There was one problem, though. Whoever had designed the ship hadn't left enough room for a man with a handful of balloons to get down the passageway. You could do it if you released some of the balloons, but the balloon man just couldn't do that. He had seen some crackers and cheese on the upper deck earlier, so he went back and ate that instead. It was good. Maybe not as good as the chef's dinner, but it was good enough. Besides, he had his balloons. That night the sunset was beautiful and it was exciting to walk along the deck. But it sure got cold quickly after that. Sea air not only makes you hungry, it makes you tired as well. He asked one of the ship's crew where his room was, and the crewman took him down a wide hall and opened the door of his cabin.

It was beautiful. They had given him one of the classiest rooms on the ship. He could see that the interior decorating was the best. And the bed looked inviting. Unfortunately, the door to the cabin was so designed that he couldn't get all the balloons in without breaking some. He tried, but it just wouldn't work.

Back on deck he found some blankets and a deck chair. He tied the balloons around his wrist and the arm of the chair and tried to sleep. The next morning he was still tired. All that day he ate crackers and cheese and that night he slept on deck again.

The next morning the balloon man received an engraved invitation from the captain of the ship. He had been invited to sit at the captain's table and enjoy the specialty of the world famous chef. He would prepare it especially for the balloon man. All that day the man watched as the crew made preparations for the evening banquet, and at 8:00 p.m. the ship's bell rang and the passengers began to go to the dining room. The man watched them go. Soon he could hear the murmur of voices, the sound of silverware, and the clink of glasses. The aroma of the food became even more enticing.

He stood at the end of the passageway for some time. Finally he walked to the back of the ship. He could still hear the dinner in progress. He reached in his pocket and felt the engraved invitation. He knew there was a special placed reserved for him at the captain's table. Then he looked up at his balloons. It was hard to do, but slowly — very, very slowly (he hadn't unclenched his hand for years) — one at time he uncurled his fingers. One by one the balloons began to drift away.

As he watched, the wind caught them and blew them out of sight. The man turned and walked down the passageway. That night, as a guest at the captain's table, he enjoyed the finest meal and the best companionship he'd ever known.

(From *More Hot Illustrations for Youth*, by Wayne Rice. Copyright 1995 by Youth Specialties. Used by permission.)

WHAT'S THE POINT?

Maybe it's time to just let go of those balloons that are keeping you from trusting Jesus; then you can enjoy the relationship with Christ that is yours for the taking.

MEDITATING ON GOD'S WORD

Psalm 125:1
"Those who trust in the LORD are like Mount Zion, which cannot be shaken but endures forever."

Ephesians 5:8
"For you were once darkness, but now you are light in the Lord. Live as children of light."

Colossians 3:5
"Put to death, therefore, whatever belongs to your earthly nature: sexual immorality, impurity, lust, evil desires, and greed, which is idolatry."

Colossians 3:8-10
"But now you must rid yourselves of all such things as these: anger, rage, malice, and filthy language from your lips. Do not lie to each other, since you have taken off your old self with its practices and have put on the new self which is being renewed in knowledge in the image of its Creator."

Hebrews 12:1
"Let us throw off everything that hinders and the sin that so easily entangles."

DIGGING DEEPER

1. Are you hanging on to a handful of balloons that keep you from being close to Jesus?

2. What are the names of your balloons? (For example: friends, bad habits, sex, popularity, possessions, pride)

3. What are you missing out on in life by holding onto the balloon instead of letting Jesus hold on to you?

4. What is one thing that hinders your spiritual walk that you can get rid of this week?

5. How is greed like idolatry (Colossians 3:5)?

6. What do you mostly daydream or think about? How do these

thoughts relate to what's of value in your life? Are these the balloons you are afraid to let go of?

7. How afraid of the dark were you when you were a child? Can you think of one vivid experience? How is darkness a good description of a life controlled by sin? Are you still in darkness spiritually? Are these balloons keeping you from the light?

8. In what sense is light a good description of a life controlled by the spirit?

9. Do you think darkness and light can exist together in a Christian?

10. What has helped you to get rid of those balloons in your life?

11. How would you describe your progress at letting go of the balloons?

12. Look at the life of Mephibosheth in Scripture. He was afraid of King David who only wanted to give him back his grandfather Saul's land. He lived his early life in poverty and he didn't have to. Are you missing out on God's blessings because you don't trust him with your life?

OBEDIENCE

SMALL BOTTLE OF URINE

A small bottle containing urine sat upon the desk of Sir William Osler, the eminent professor of medicine at Oxford University. Sitting before him was a class of young, wide-eyed medical students, listening to his lecture on the importance of observing details. To emphasize his point, he announced: "This bottle contains a sample for analysis. It's often possible by tasting it to determine the disease from which the patient suffers."

He then dipped a finger into the fluid and brought it into his mouth. He continued speaking: "Now I am going to pass the bottle around. Each of you please do exactly as I did. Perhaps we can learn the importance of this technique and diagnose the case."

The bottle made its way from row to row, each student gingerly poking his finger in and bravely sampling the contents with a frown. Dr. Osler then retrieved the bottle and startled the students by saying, "Gentlemen, now you will understand what I mean when I speak about details. Had you been observant, you would have seen that I put my index finger in the bottle but my middle finger into my mouth!"

(From *Hot Illustrations for Youth*, by Wayne Rice. Copyright 1994 by Youth Specialties. Used by permission.)

WHAT'S THE POINT?

Many people live their lives just like the students in Professor Osler's class. They think they have life all figured out, but they have forgotten one important detail: the need to be obedient to Christ's plan of salvation. As a result of their disobedience, life is toxic and bitter.

God doesn't hide from us or try to deceive us as Professor Osler did his students. The Bible clearly gives us instructions for coming to Christ and for living a life with purpose and meaning.

MEDITATING ON GOD'S WORD

Genesis 22:18
"...And through your offspring all nations on earth will be blessed, because you have obeyed me."

2 Kings 5:13-14
"Naaman's servants went to him and said, "My father, if the prophet had told you to do some great thing, would you not have done it? How much more, then, when he tells you, 'Wash and be cleansed.'!" So he went down and dipped himself in the Jordan seven times, as the man of God had told him, and his flesh was restored and became clean as that of a young boy."

2 Kings 21:8
"I will not again make the feet of the Israelites wander from the land I gave their forefathers, if only they will be careful to do everything I commanded them and will keep the whole Law that my servant Moses gave them."

Psalm 34:8
"Taste and see that the LORD is good; blessed is the man who takes refuge in him."

John 14:15
"If you love me, you will obey what I command."

Acts 5:29
"We must obey God rather than men!"

DIGGING DEEPER

1. As a child, whom did you go to for counsel? What do you remember about that person? What was the most helpful advice they gave you?

2. How are love and obedience connected?

3. How has your love for God and your obedience to him changed in the last six months?

4. Naaman was hesitating to do what God told him to do because it wasn't what he was expecting God to say. Have you ever felt God's plans were different than yours? What did you do?

5. What are some of "the little details" from God's word that you need to work on obeying?

6. At school, how much does peer pressure influence your decisions? How much does God's word? What is Acts 5:29 telling us?

7. If obedience brings good results and disobedience brings negative results, why do we continue to disobey?

8. What do these verses say about God's authority in the believer's life?

9. What is the ultimate authority in your life? When does this create problems for you? What can you do to overcome these problems?

GRACE

RAISIN IN THE SUN

Lorraine Hansburg has a delightful play called, "Raisin in the Sun." It's about a black family in Harlem. The father dies and leaves about $10,000 to the family. The mother says this will allow her to fulfill her dream. Her dream is to have a little house in North Jersey with window boxes and flowers.

The son of the household begs for the money. This young man has never had a chance, never a break, never had a decent job. He has a friend, and with the $10,000 he and his friend could go into business. They have a deal and they could make a lot of money and do good things for the family. He begs and pleads. At first his mother doesn't want to give it to him. But how can she deny her boy, her son, who has never gotten a chance? So the young man gets the money.

You can imagine what happens. His friend takes the money and leaves town. The son returns home battered and beaten, embarrassed and destroyed. Then, when he comes home, his sister Benetha tears him up, puts him down, and has contempt for him for having been so stupid as to be ripped off like this and destroy the family's hopes.

The mother speaks to Benetha: "I thought I taught you to love him." Benetha says, "Love him? There's nothing left to love." And mom says, "There's always something left to love, and if you ain't learned that you ain't learned nothing. Have you cried for that boy today? I don't mean for yourself and for your family because we lost that money. I mean for him, for what he has been through, what it has done to him. Child, child, when do you think is the time to love somebody the most? When they have done good and made things easy for everybody? Well, you ain't through learning, 'cause that ain't the time at all. It's when he is at his lowest and can't believe in himself 'cause the world done whipped him so. When you start measuring someone, child, measure him right. Measure him right. Be sure you know what hills and valleys he's been through to get to wherever he is."

(Adapted from a message given by Tony Campolo at the Youth Specialties National Convention in 1993.)

WHAT'S THE POINT?

I don't know what you call that. The Bible calls it grace. It's when you don't deserve love and you get love, when you don't deserve to be cared for and you are cared for. God loves you, not only when you've done something good. "Where sin increased..." what does the Scripture say? That "grace increased all the more" (Romans 5:20). He loves you. He creates a love that enables you to love that other person no matter what that person does. Do you understand that? That's why Christianity has an answer that the world will never grasp until it grasps Jesus.

MEDITATING ON GOD'S WORD

Psalm 84:11 (NCV)
"...The Lord gives us kindness and honor. He does not hold back anything good from those whose lives are innocent."

Romans 9:16
"It does not, therefore, depend on man's desire or effort, but on God's mercy."

1 Timothy 1:14
"The grace of our Lord was poured out on me abundantly."

Titus 2:11
"For the grace of God that brings salvation has appeared to all men."

Titus 3:5

"...He saved us, not because of righteous things we had done, but because of his mercy."

Titus 3:7

"...So that, having been justified by his grace..."

DIGGING DEEPER

1. What do you find most interesting about your family background?

2. If you had been the mother, would you have given the son the money?

3. How would you have responded to what happened?

4. What instances in your life have helped you to comprehend God's grace a little better?

5. How do you treat people when they mess something up for you?

6. What hinders you from being a more gracious person?

7. In what ways is the Apostle Paul's life an example of God's grace and patience?

8. When has your faith come closest to being shipwrecked? What did God do to save your faith?

9. How is your life an example of God's grace to others?

10. What will you do this week to show God's grace to others?

11. How does understanding what you used to be and what God has done for you encourage you now?

12. Why is it difficult to love the unlovely? Do you think someone may look at you as being unlovely? How does that make you feel?

DETERMINATION

THE FOUR MINUTE MILE

In the 1950s, an athlete by the name of Roger Bannister was one of the best and fastest mile runners from England. He was picked to win the Olympics. That was in the days when they said it was humanly impossible to run a mile in less than 4 minutes; that the human body could not endure that. Now if you know anything about track, you know that today you cannot even participate in world class running unless you can run the mile in under 4 minutes. But in the 1950s, they said it couldn't be done.

Roger Bannister came in a disappointing third, so he thought he would quit running and devote all of his time to his medical studies. His coach got ahold of him and said, "Roger, you are the best miler I have ever seen. You have what it takes to do what everyone has said cannot be done — to break the 4 minute barrier."

He took the challenge of his coach and set out to do it. His schedule was sleep, eat, study, and work out six hours every day. He did it for months. One day he said to his teammates, "Today I'm going to do it."

Four times around the track equals a mile. Chris Chadway set the pace for the first two laps. Roger has said that on the fourth lap his legs felt like rubber, his lungs felt like they were going to burst. He said to himself, "Roger, you got an outstanding time, just coast in and you will probably set a record." But then there was that voice in him that said, "This is no time to coast, but to kick in." So, instead of slackening the pace, he began to sprint.

On the last curve, he could see the finish line with his coach behind it. He closed his eyes, he clenched his fist, he bit his lips, and ran with every ounce of energy in his body. He fell across the tape into the arms of his coach. His time: 3:59:07. He did it. He did what everyone else said was impossible.

WHAT'S THE POINT?

Determination is what separates the winners from the losers. Roger Bannister was about to give up until he felt the determination to push beyond the limits of his time. Society tells us that it is okay to just coast our way to the finish line. When you are in a race, wouldn't you rather listen to that inner voice telling you to kick in?

MEDITATING ON GOD'S WORD

Numbers 14:24
"But because my servant Caleb has a different spirit and follows me wholeheartedly, I will bring him into the land he went to, and his descendants will inherit it."

Proverbs 28:1
"...The righteous are as bold as a lion."

Luke 21:19
"By standing firm, you will gain life."

1 Corinthians 9:24
"...Run in such a way as to get the prize."

1 Corinthians 15:58
"Therefore, my dear brothers, stand firm. Let nothing move you. Always give yourselves fully to the work of the Lord, because you know that your labor in the Lord in not in vain."

Galatians 6:9
"Let us not become weary in doing good, for at the proper time we will reap a harvest if we do not give up."

Philippians 3:13-14
"...Straining toward what is ahead, I press on toward the goal."

2 Timothy 4:17
"But the Lord stood at my side and gave me strength."

Titus 2:14
"...Eager to do what is good."

Hebrews 6:12
"We do not want you to become lazy."

Hebrews 10:23-24
"Let us hold unswervingly to the hope we profess, for he who promised us is faithful. And let us consider how we may spur one another on toward love and good deeds."

Hebrews 10:36
"You need to persevere so that when you have done the will of God, you will receive what he has promised."

Hebrews 12:1
"...Let us run with perseverance the race marked out for us."

James 5:11
"As you know, we consider blessed those who have persevered."

DIGGING DEEPER

1. Why do we settle for second best sometimes?

2. Do you see yourself as someone who has strong determination and willpower? Is this a good quality? Why?

3. How can you help others to see the importance of putting their mind to something and actually doing it?

4. Why do you think that God looks more favorably on those who persevere and are determined to follow through?

5. What is one time in your life where you really had to be strong in your determination?

6. How would you have felt if you were in Roger Bannister's shoes? Would you have done the same thing?

7. What is at the top of your want list? How will it change your life?

8. How have you experienced strength and joy in the midst of a trial? What is the great trial you are facing now?

9. Why is it important to persevere in the face of suffering? How is Job a good example?

10. How would people who know you rate you on determination? What part do you need to work on?

11. How do your friends spur you on in your spiritual race?

12. What discourages you most in your spiritual journey? What/ who helps keep you going?

13. If God would whisper "Press on" to you, what would he be referring to?

COMPLETE SURRENDER

DUDLEY TYNG

In the middle of the 1800s, a man named Dudley Tyng was one of the many preachers responsible for a revival in the city of Philadelphia. Several churches were having thousands of people come. Tyng was only 29 years old, but when he would preach, people would get so moved they would be on their knees before he finished. One Sunday at a noon meeting at the YMCA, five thousand men were listening to him, with three thousand on their knees in prayer, and one thousand responding by committing their hearts and lives to Christ.

One Monday morning, Dudley Tyng went out to help a farmer shell corn. He got his arm caught in the corn sheller and it ripped it right out of its socket. They rushed him right to the hospital. Medical facilities not being what they are today, the arm became infected and young Dudley Tyng was dying.

As he was on his deathbed, all the pastors from the city, including his father, came to his hospital room. Dudley Tyng tried to sing, "Rock of Ages," but he was so weak he couldn't finish it. Before he died, he motioned for his dad to come near and this is what he said, "Dad, tell them to stand up for Jesus." A fellow pastor and a close friend of Dudley's, George Duffield, was so moved by that, he went back and preached a sermon titled, "Stand Up for Jesus." He concluded it with a poem. The poem was printed for distribution in Sunday Schools.

Several years later, George Duffield was out at an army barracks and off in the distance he heard a group of soldiers singing his poem to a tune. It was the first he realized he had written the words to a hymn. His poem was:

> Stand up, stand up for Jesus,
> Ye soldiers of the cross.
> Lift high his royal banner,
> It must not suffer loss.
> From victory unto victory,
> His army shall he lead.
> 'Til every foe is vanquished,
> And Christ is Lord indeed.

The third verse goes:

> Stand up, stand up for Jesus,
> Stand in his strength alone.
> The arm of flesh will fail you,
> You dare not trust your own.

WHAT'S THE POINT?

Even on his deathbed, Dudley Tyng realized that the only thing that mattered in life was to live completely for Jesus. All too often in life, we are told to go along with the majority and forget about our own convictions.

MEDITATING ON GOD'S WORD

Matthew 4:19
"Come, follow me," Jesus said, "and I will make you fishers of men."

Matthew 16:25
"For whoever wants to save his life will lose it, but whoever loses his life for me will find it."

Luke 9:23
"If anyone would come after me, he must deny himself and take up his cross daily and follow me."

Ephesians 6:14
"Stand firm then, with the belt of truth buckled around your waist..."

2 Timothy 3:12
"...Everyone who wants to live a godly life in Christ Jesus will be persecuted."

1 John 3:16
"...We ought to lay down our lives..."

DIGGING DEEPER

1. Has something ever happened in your life that inspired you to surrender your life completely to Christ?

2. How would your life be different if you were a preacher with the charisma that Tyng had?

3. What would you like your last words on your deathbed to be?

4. What thing(s) in your life would you die for?

5. When you die, what do you want to be remembered for? What do you want written on your tombstone?

6. Who has the biggest positive influence on your life? Why?

7. If Jesus came by your school and called you like he did the early disciples, what would you do?

8. What are some tough things that lie ahead for you?

9. What does it mean, specifically for you, to deny self, take up your cross, and follow Jesus?

10. What are some areas in your life that God is calling you to die to? What is hardest about giving up this area of your life?

11. Do you think it's true that everyone who wants to live a godly life will be persecuted? Why or why not? How does this make you feel?

FORGIVENESS

LEONARDO DA VINCI

There is an old tradition that at the time that Leonardo da Vinci painted "The Last Supper," he had an enemy who was a fellow painter. Da Vinci had a bitter argument with this man and despised him. When da Vinci painted the face of Judas Iscariot at the table with Jesus, he used the face of his enemy so that it would be present for ages as the man who betrayed Jesus. He took delight while painting this picture in knowing that others would actually notice the face of his enemy on Judas.

The legend goes on to reveal that as da Vinci worked on the faces of the other disciples, he often tried to paint the face of Jesus, but couldn't make any progress. Da Vinci felt frustrated and confused. In time he realized what was wrong. His hatred for the other painter was holding him back from finishing the face of Jesus. Only after making peace with his fellow painter and repainting the face of Judas was he able to paint the face of Jesus and complete his masterpiece.

(From *Hot Illustrations for Youth*, by Wayne Rice. Copyright 1994 by Youth Specialties. Used by permission.)

WHAT'S THE POINT?

One of the reasons we may have a hard time accepting the forgiveness of God is that we find it hard to forgive others. If you want your relationship with Jesus to be all that it should be, forgive your enemies and do all you can to demonstrate Christ's love to them.

MEDITATING ON GOD'S WORD

1 Kings 8:50
"And forgive your people, who have sinned against you; forgive all the offenses they have committed against you...."

Matthew 6:14-15
"For if you forgive men when they sin against you, your heavenly Father will also forgive you. But if you do not forgive men their sins, your Father will not forgive your sins."

Matthew 18:35
"This is how my heavenly Father will treat each of you unless you forgive your brother from your heart."

2 Corinthians 2:10
"If you forgive anyone, I also forgive him."

Ephesians 4:32
"Be kind and compassionate to one another, forgiving each other, just as in Christ God forgave you."

Colossians 3:13
"Bear with each other and forgive whatever grievances you may have against one another."

1 John 2:9
"Anyone who claims to be in the light but hates his brother is still in the darkness."

DIGGING DEEPER

1. Have you ever experienced this kind of bitterness towards a person? Explain.

2. How do you feel when you go to a person and ask for forgiveness?

3. How would you have felt if you were da Vinci?

4. Do you find it hard to accept God's forgiveness? Explain.

5. Whom if anyone do you need to forgive? What specific steps can you take to forgive him or her?

6. How does it make you feel when someone else has to ask you for your forgiveness?

7. What happens when hatred is adopted as a lifestyle?

8. How does walking in the light of Jesus improve your fellowship with other people?

9. How do prayer and forgiveness go together?

10. To whom have you offered much forgiveness? What has resulted from your forgiving attitude?

11. Who has extended the most forgiveness to you?

12. What is the best way to forgive people who don't know they have wronged you?

13. How important is forgiveness to health and personal wholeness? Why?

14. Why should Christians forgive each other? What should motivate us to do this?

15. When is it hardest for you to forgive? Why?

19

GREED

CRANKY OLD RICH MAN

Once there was an old rich man with a cranky, miserable attitude. He visited a rabbi one day to see if the rabbi might be able to help him discover what was wrong with his life.

After the two men talked together for a while, the rabbi thought of a good way to illustrate to the rich man the problem with his life. Taking the man by the hand, he led him over to the window. He asked him to look out the window and tell him what he saw. The man stood there for a moment before saying, "I see some men and women and a few children."

"Fine," said the rabbi. Once more he led the rich man by the hand across the room to the mirror. "Now look and tell me what you see."

The man frowned and said, "Well, obviously I see myself."

"Interesting," the rabbi replied. "The window is made of glass, and the mirror is also made of glass. But the glass of the mirror has been covered with silver. As soon as you add the silver, you cease to see others and instead see only yourself."

(From *Hot Illustrations for Youth*, by Wayne Rice. Copyright 1994 by Youth Specialties. Used by permission.)

WHAT'S THE POINT?

Like the old man, if you "cover your life with silver" (money, wealth), you'll be unhappy. Unhappiness overtakes you because you stop thinking of others, and you begin to think only of yourself. The way people feel happy is by loving God and loving others more than themselves. No one is more miserable than a vain, self-centered person.

MEDITATING ON GOD'S WORD

Psalm 49:16-17
"Do not be overawed when a man grows rich, when the splendor of his house increases; for he will take nothing with him when he dies; his splendor will not descend with him."

Proverbs 15:27
"A greedy man brings trouble to his family."

Proverbs 28:11
"A rich man may be wise in his own eyes, but a poor man who has discernment sees through him."

Jeremiah 9:23
"…Let not…the rich man boast of his riches."

Ezekiel 7:19
"Their silver and gold will not be able to save them in the day of the LORD's wrath."

Matthew 16:26
"What good will it be for a man if he gains the whole world, yet forfeits his soul?"

Luke 16:13
"…You cannot serve both God and money."

2 Timothy 3:1-2
"…In the last days, people will be lovers of themselves, lovers of money."

THE APPLICATION(DIGGING DEEPER

1. How would you have answered this rich man?

2. What is your general opinion of money? Is it good, bad, evil, etc?

3. Where (besides in God's love) have you tried to look for happiness?

4. If you could put a monetary figure to being rich or wealthy, what would it be?

5. What is the difference between these two statements:
   1. "Money is the root of all evil."
   2. "The love of money is the root of all evil."

6. Have you ever met someone who you have considered to be very wealthy? How was that person alike or different from the rich man in this illustration?

7. Look up these people in Scripture who had an unhealthy love of money:
   Balaam (Numbers 22; Jude 11; 2 Peter 2:15)
   Achan (Joshua 7:21)
   Ahab (1 Kings 21: 2-16)
   Judas (Matthew 26:15-16)
   Demas (2 Timothy 4:10)

8. Has money gotten in the way of any of your relationships?

9. The United States is the wealthiest country in the world. What do you think God wants to say to us regarding money?

10. How much does money control decisions you make about your life?

20

EXPECTATIONS

THE JIGSAW PUZZLE

A family had a hobby of putting together jigsaw puzzles. The father regularly brought home puzzles of greater and greater difficulty. One night he presented his family with a puzzle of over one thousand pieces. Immediately they tackled it. After an hour, however, the family was frustrated. No matter how hard they tried, they couldn't get the puzzle started.

The father then discovered that he had accidentally switched the box top with the top from another puzzle. The picture they were looking at wasn't the puzzle they were working on.

(From *Hot Illustrations for Youth*, by Wayne Rice. Copyright 1994 by Youth Specialties. Used by permission.)

WHAT'S THE POINT?

We may feel frustrated with God because he doesn't live up to the expectations we have of him. Sometimes we feel frustrated with the church because it doesn't match up with the ideal church that we have in mind. We're often frustrated with others because they fall short of expectations that we have of them.

Perhaps we should consider whether the problem in all these cases is that we are basing our expectations on a distorted view — of God or of the church or of others. Perhaps our expectations are unrealistic and can never be realized because we've been looking at the picture on the wrong box top.

We may also feel frustrated with ourselves because we don't believe we live up to what others want from us or even what we think God wants from us. More often than not, though, our problem is trying to make ourselves into someone else's image or change ourselves to fit someone else's standard for us. God created us each to be different. We all have our own "box-top picture" and the only way we can ever be successful in life is to be ourselves, allowing God to use us just the way we are.

MEDITATING ON GOD'S WORD

Haggai 1:9
"You expected much, but see, it turned out to be little..."

Acts 20:30
"...Men will arise and distort the truth in order to draw away disciples after them."

Romans 8:29
"...Be conformed to the likeness of his Son..."

Romans 12:2
"Do not conform any longer to the pattern of this world, but be transformed by the renewing of your mind..."

2 Corinthians 4:4
"The god of this age has blinded the minds of unbelievers, so that they cannot see the light of the gospel of the glory of Christ, who is the image of God."

2 Peter 3:16
"His letters contain some things that are hard to understand, which ignorant and unstable people distort, as they do the other Scriptures, to their own destruction."

DIGGING DEEPER

1. Explain a time when you felt like God let you down.

2. What sort of unrealistic expectations have you placed upon yourself? God? Others?

3. When were some times that you really knew that someone was trying to draw you away from God or distort your view of him?

4. Explain a time when you let someone else down by not living up to their expectations. How did it make you feel?

5. Is it difficult for you to recognize the truth? Explain.

6. How do you feel when you discover that you've been following in the wrong direction?

7. Do you feel like you would like to be someone else at times? Who? Why?

FOCUS

THE LAST SUPPER

According to legend, one of the reasons "The Last Supper" took four years to complete was that when da Vinci was almost finished, a friend commented on how incredibly moving the painting was — especially the silver cup on the table. He said how beautiful it was and how his eyes were immediately drawn to it. Da Vinci got so angry that he immediately painted over the cup, blotting it out. The focus of the painting was to be Jesus, not the cup. All attention had to be drawn to him; anything that detracted had to be removed.

(From *Hot Illustrations for Youth*, by Wayne Rice. Copyright 1994 by Youth Specialties. Used by permission.)

WHAT'S THE POINT?

What's the focus of your life? We need to remove anything that comes before Christ or hinders us from serving him. Christ must be the center of our lives.

MEDITATING ON GOD'S WORD

Psalm 25:15
"My eyes are ever on the Lord."

Psalm 141:8
"But my eyes are fixed on you, O Sovereign Lord..."

Proverbs 4:25
"Let your eyes look straight ahead, fix your gaze directly before you."

1 Corinthians 9:26
"Therefore, I do not run like a man running aimlessly."

Philippians 1:21
"For me, to live is Christ..."

Philippians 3:14
"I press on toward the goal..."

Hebrews 2:1
"We must pay more careful attention, therefore, to what we have heard, so that we do not drift away."

Hebrews 12:1-2
"Therefore, since we are surrounded by such a great cloud of witnesses, let us throw off everything that hinders and the sin that so easily entangles, and let us run with perseverance the race marked out for us. Let us fix our eyes on Jesus, the author and perfecter of our faith, who for the joy set before him endured the cross, scorning its shame, and sat down at the right hand of the throne of God."

1 Peter 2:1
"Therefore, rid yourself of all malice and all deceit, hypocrisy, envy, and slander of every kind."

DIGGING DEEPER

1. What does it mean to fix our eyes on Jesus?

2. What have you discovered that helps you keep your eyes fixed on Jesus?

3. What things in your life have caused you to lose focus, to drift from God's truth? How did you pull yourself out of it? Who helped?

4. How do you refocus when things seem to be hindering you?

5. Have you caused others to lose focus? Explain.

6. What does Paul mean when he writes "For me to live is Christ"?

7. If not from Christ, where else might you go to attempt to receive joy?

NONCONFORMITY

THE SCARECROW

Being different is the poetry of life. L. Frank Baum followed up his very successful book *The Wizard of Oz* with a sequel entitled *The Land of Oz* written in 1904. He featured two of his characters from the previous book, the Scarecrow and the Tin Woodsman. In one scene, the scarecrow is talking to a character named Jack Pumpkinhead. Jack Pumpkinhead had just received from the Tin Woodsman a new beautifully carved wooden leg taken from a mahogany table. It struck Jack Pumpkinhead as being odd that he now had such a unique body.

"It seems strange" said he, as he watched the Tin Woodsman work, "that my left leg should be the most elegant and substantial part of me."

"That proves that you are unusual," returned the scarecrow; "and I am convinced that the only people worthy of consideration in this world are the unusual ones. For the common folks are like the leaves of a tree, and live and die unnoticed."

WHAT'S THE POINT?

As we see in life, most people live and die completely unnoticed. Those that are noticed didn't let the world squeeze them into its mold. They were different and unique. There are not two snowflakes, fingerprints, voices, or personalities alike. God likes variety and diversity. Be the unique person he wants you to be.

MEDITATING ON GOD'S WORD

1 Samuel 10:6
"...You will be changed into a different person."

Romans 12:2
"Do not conform any longer to the pattern of this world, but be transformed by the renewing of your mind."

1 Corinthians 4:7
"For who makes you different from anyone else?"

1 Corinthians 10:31
"So whether you eat or drink or whatever you do, do it all for the glory of God."

Ephesians 1:11
"In him we were also chosen, having been predestined according to the plan of him who works out everything in conformity with the purpose of his will."

Titus 2:14 (KJV)
"Who gave himself for us, that he might redeem us from all iniquity, and purify unto himself a peculiar people, zealous of good works."

1 Peter 1:14
"...Do not conform to the evil desires you had when you lived in ignorance."

1 Peter 2:9 (KJV)
"But you are a chosen generation...a peculiar people."

DIGGING DEEPER

1. Do you even agree with the scarecrow's statement? Why or why not?

2. List some other people who stand out to you as being different and/or unusual in either a good or bad way.

3. What does it mean to be "transformed"?

4. What does it mean to be a "peculiar people"?

5. Would you rather die being unusual but noticed, or unnoticed but usual?

6. Based upon which one of the above you'd like to be, how do you plan on living to achieve that goal?

7. Evaluate yourself and your life in its current state. Which category are you in now?

COMMITMENT

PRINCE OF GRANADA

The prince of Granada, an heir to the Spanish crown, was sentenced to life in solitary confinement in Madrid's ancient prison called "The Place of the Skull." The fearful, dirty, and dreary nature of the place earned it the name. Everyone knew that once you were in, you would never come out alive. The prince was given one book to read the entire time — the Bible. With only one book to read, he read it over hundreds and hundreds of times. The book became his constant companion.

After thirty-three years of imprisonment, he died. When they came in to clean out his cell, they found some notes he had written using nails to mark the soft stones of the prison walls. The notations were of this sort: Psalms 118:8 is the middle verse of the Bible; Ezra 7:21 contains all the letters of the alphabet except the letter j; the ninth verse of the eighth chapter of Esther is the longest verse in the Bible.

When Scot Udell originally noted these facts in an article in *Psychology Today*, he noted the oddity of an individual who spent thirty-three years of his life studying what some have described as the greatest book of all time yet could only glean trivia. From all we know, he never made any religious or spiritual commitment to Christ, but he became an expert at Bible trivia.

(From *Hot Illustrations for Youth*, by Wayne Rice. Copyright 1994 by Youth Specialties. Used by permission.)

WHAT'S THE POINT?

There's a difference between knowing facts about God, Jesus Christ, and the Bible, and allowing God to change you from the inside out. Many people grow up knowing a lot about Christianity but never have committed their lives to Christ.

MEDITATING ON GOD'S WORD

Exodus 33:13
"If you are pleased with me, teach me your ways so I may know you and continue to find favor with you."

Joshua 24:15
"But as for me and my household, we will serve the LORD."

Ruth 1:16
"Your people will be my people and your God [will be] my God."

1 Samuel 17:46
"…The whole world will know that there is a God…"

1 Kings 18:21
"How long will you waver between two opinions? If the LORD is God, follow him; but if Baal is God, follow him."

John 4:42
"…We know that this man really is the Savior of the world."

John 17:8
"For I gave them the words you gave me and they accepted them…they believed you sent me."

Philippians 3:10
"I want to know Christ…"

2 Thessalonians 1:8
"He will punish those who do not know God and do not obey the gospel of our Lord Jesus."

1 John 4:14
"If anyone acknowledges that Jesus is the Son of God, God lives in him, and he in God."

DIGGING DEEPER

1. Why do you think that the prince looked at the Bible as only a matter of trivia?

2. Has your faith ever resembled that of the prince's faith? What did you do to change it?

3. What are people missing who look at the Bible as only good literature?

4. What mindsets and actions in your life have limited the influence of God's word in your life?

5. Who helped you the most to come to know Christ? How?

6. In your own spiritual pilgrimage, how much have you been influenced by God's word?

7. What, for you, would be the worst thing about not knowing Jesus? Why?

8. Have you allowed God to change you from the inside out?

9. In what ways do you desire to know God even more?

GENEROSITY

QUEEN OF ENGLAND'S UMBRELLA

The queen of England often visits Bob Morrow Castle. On one occasion when she was walking by herself, it started to rain. She rushed to the shelter of the nearest cottage. A lady came to the door who was really ticked off that someone would bother her at that time in the morning. She opened the door a few inches and barked, "What do you want?"

The queen didn't introduce herself. She merely asked, "May I borrow an umbrella?"

"Just a minute," grumbled the woman. She slammed the door, was gone for a moment, and returned bringing the rattiest umbrella she could find, one with broken ribs and small holes. She pushed it through the door and said, "Here." The queen of England thanked her and went on her way with the ragged umbrella.

The next morning, the queen's full escort, dressed in full uniform, pulled up in front of the cottage. One of the escorts knocked on the door and returned the umbrella to the woman saying, "Madam, the Queen of England thanks you." As he walked away he heard her mutter, "If I'd only known, I'd have given her my best."

(From *Hot Illustrations for Youth*, by Wayne Rice. Copyright 1994 by Youth Specialties. Used by permission.)

WHAT'S THE POINT?

Some day we'll all stand before the King of heaven and some will be heard to mutter, "If I'd only known, I'd have given you my best." The fact is, we do know, and yet many of us still give Christ the scraps, the leftovers, whatever costs us the least.

Because God loved us, he gave us his very best, his Son. Can we give him anything less than our best?

MEDITATING ON GOD'S WORD

1 Samuel 12:24
"But be sure to fear the LORD and serve him faithfully with all your heart..."

Matthew 25:40
"...I tell you the truth, whatever you did for one of the least of these brothers of mine, you did for me."

2 Corinthians 8:7
"...Excel in this grace of giving."

Galatians 5:13
"...Serve one another in love."

Galatians 6:2
"Carry each other's burdens, and in this way you will fulfill the law of Christ."

Galatians 6:10
"Therefore, as we have opportunity, let us do good to all people..."

Hebrews 13:2
"Do not forget to entertain strangers, for by so doing some people have entertained angels without knowing it."

DIGGING DEEPER

1. Has there ever been a time when you have withheld your best? Describe?

2. If you were the Queen, how would you have responded to the woman?

3. Why do people try to justify themselves and give Christ less than he deserves?

4. How does it make you feel when you know that someone is not giving you their best?

5. If you were the woman, what would you have done when the Queen's escort came to your door?

6. How does it make you feel to know that there are some who will say to God, "If I had only known"?

7. What is your most vivid memory of helping someone else?

8. What sort of burdens do your friends carry? How could you help them with these burdens?

9. If you had a million dollars to give away, who would you give it to? Why?

10. How important do you think generosity is to the church? To the individual?

11. How does the use of money indicate priorities?

12. How do you decide how much to give?

FREEDOM

JEHOIACHIN

No Longer a Prisoner

Picture a sumptuous banquet: the array of kings and dignitaries, the pageantry, the perilous protocol, and the dazzling splendor.

From an obscure door at the side of the room, a slight figure enters. He is stooped. His psyche, the inner self, is also bowed. He wants no recognition, only a seat at the edge of the splendor. It is enough that he is free.

A stir ripples across the great chamber as the new visitor is intercepted. Instead of being placed at the side of the banquet, the frail figure is given a seat above the other kings present there.

For thirty years, he had been banished to solitary confinement. Year after year, he languished there until a new king came into power. One of the king's first acts was to go to the prison, lift up the head of this man, and whisper "You are free." He invited him to put off his prison garb and dine at the royal table.

WHAT'S THE POINT?

This is a true story from 2 Kings. The prisoner set free was Jehoiachin, but the parallels between this man and us are apparent. We once were held prisoner by our human weaknesses and sin. It was only when Jesus defeated death on the cross and chose out of his grace to free us that we were able to be free. Above all of that, though, he invited us to sup with him, not like an ex-prisoner, but like royalty. 2 Kings 25:29 tells us that "Jehoiachin put off his prison garments, and for the rest of his life...he dined regularly at the king's table." Jesus invites you to be a lifetime guest at his incredible feast of freedom.

MEDITATING ON GOD'S WORD

Matthew 25:34
"Then the king will say to those on his right, 'Come you who are blessed by my Father; take your inheritance, the kingdom prepared for you since the creation of the world.'"

John 8:32, 36
"Then you will know the truth and the truth will set you free...So if the Son sets you free, you will be free indeed."

Romans 8:2
"...Because through Christ Jesus the law of the spirit of life set me free from the law of sin and death."

1 Corinthians 7:22-23
"For he who was a slave when he was called by the Lord is the Lord's freedman...you were bought with a price. Do not become slaves of men."

Galatians 5:1
"It is for freedom that Christ has set us free. Stand firm, then, and do not let yourselves be burdened again by a yoke of slavery."

Philippians 3:20
"Our citizenship is in heaven..."

1 Peter 2:16
"Live as free men, but do not use your freedom as a cover-up for evil; live as servants of God."

DIGGING DEEPER

1. When in your life have you felt the freest? Why?

2. How and from what is the Christian set free?

3. What price did Jesus pay for your freedom? How does that make you feel?

4. How are you going to praise God for setting you free?

5. If you could write a thank-you letter to Jesus, what would you say?

6. What are some areas of pride that keep you from enjoying God's blessing? How has God been breaking down those barriers?

7. God has a feast prepared for you right now. Are you eating or are you just watching?

8. What or who is "truth"? How will this set us free?

9. What freedoms do you have that you take for granted?

SENSITIVITY

I CAN'T HOLD ON ANY LONGER

The climactic event at Detroit's Cobo Hall exhibition of Ringling Brothers Barnum and Bailey Circus was the high-wire act of the Wallenda family, or the Flying Wallendas, as they were known. They were among the greatest tightwire walkers in all of circus history.

One of their acts was walking the tightrope in the formation of a four-level pyramid. Four or five men formed the first level, two or three men made up the second level, two more were on the third, and finally a little girl topped the pyramid. Maintaining this four-level pyramid, they would make their way across the tightrope from one side of the arena to the other. It was incredible and unprecedented. They did it night after night, month after month around the world.

One particular evening, as the show came to its conclusion, the four-level pyramid was about to start. The audience tensed in anticipation, sitting in total silence in the dark arena. The spotlights picked the Wallendas out of the air as they started moving across the wire. About two-thirds of the way across, however, one of the men on the first level, young Dede Wallenda, began to tremble in his knees. He cried out in German, "I cannot hold on any longer!" With that, he crumbled, and the entire pyramid collapsed. Several of the Wallendas fell to the floor many feet below. Some were crippled for life and one died.

(From *Hot Illustrations for Youth*, by Wayne Rice. Copyright 1994 by Youth Specialties. Used by permission.)

WHAT'S THE POINT?

Have you ever felt like Dede Wallenda? The pressures of school, homework, parents, family, or friends weigh down on you until you feel like yelling, "Help! I cannot hold on any longer!" While facing those times, we need to surround ourselves with loving friends and hold on to Christ. That's what the church is all about. The church doesn't exist to put additional pressure on us, but to support us and provide us with the help we need to survive in the world. When you feel like your knees are about to buckle, come to Christ and his church.

MEDITATING ON GOD'S WORD

John 14:27
"Peace I leave with you...Do not let your hearts be troubled and do not be afraid."

John 16:33
"...In this world, you will have trouble. But take heart! I have overcome the world."

Philippians 4:7
"And the peace of God, which transcends all understanding, will guard your hearts and your minds in Christ Jesus."

1 Peter 5:10
"And the God of all grace, who called you to his eternal glory in Christ, after you have suffered a little while, will himself restore you and make you strong, firm, and steadfast."

1 John 4:4
"The one who is in you is greater than the one who is in the world."

DIGGING DEEPER

1. When was a time you just couldn't hold on any longer?

2. What are the top five things that stress you out?

3. What mostly robs you of peace?

4. How peaceful are you on a scale of one to ten? What role has pain played in your life? How has it changed your life?

5. What area of your life is least peaceful right now?

6. What puzzling or troubling situation do you need to bring to Jesus?

7. What promise from these verses mean the most to you?

8. What can you do to remind you of God's peace during your times of stress?

9. Do the people around add to your stress or help with it?

10. Read Luke 10:25-37 (the story of the Good Samaritan) and think of three ways you can bring peace to a troubled person this week.

27

CONSISTENCY

THE DONKEY, THE MAN,

AND THE BOY

An ancient story is told about a father and his son who were walking along a road one day with their donkey. Soon they met a man who told them how foolish they were to walk when they had a donkey that could be ridden. So the father and son hopped on.

They hadn't gone very far when another man criticized them for both riding a donkey. They were too heavy for it, he contended, and were being inhumane. So the boy got off.

It wasn't long before a third traveler accused the father of being inconsiderate because he made his son walk while he rode. So the two switched places.

Soon they met another person who charged that the son was not being thoughtful of his father, who was so much older than he.

When last seen, the two were trudging down the road carrying the donkey.

WHAT'S THE POINT?

There is an old rock song that says, "You can't please everyone, so you gotta please yourself." Who do you try to please? If you listen to the crowd and try to dance to their tune, you will always be frustrated. If you are overly sensitive to the opinions and criticisms of others, you will end up carrying a needless burden of guilt and inadequacy. And if you just try to please yourself, you will become egocentric and selfish.

That's why as Christians, we seek to please God, not other people. Ultimately, our accountability is to God. There is an old saying that says "dance with the one who brought you." God brought you into this world.

MEDITATING ON GOD'S WORD

Matthew 6:24
"No one can serve two masters."

Romans 12:2
"Do not conform any longer to the pattern of this world, but be transformed by the renewing of your mind."

1 Corinthians 3:19
"For the wisdom of this world is foolishness in God's sight."

1 Corinthians 10:21
"You cannot drink the cup of the Lord and the cup of demons too."

Galatians 1:10
"Am I now trying to win the approval of men or of God…If I were still trying to please men I would not be a servant of Christ."

Colossians 1:10
"And we pray this in order that you may live a life worthy of the Lord and may please him in every way…"

1 Thessalonians 2:4
"We are not trying to please men but God, who tests our hearts."

James 1:8
"He is a double-minded man, unstable in all he does."

James 4:4,7
"Don't you know that friendship with the world is hatred toward God…Submit yourselves, then, to God."

1 John 2:15
"Do not love the world or anything in the world. If anyone loves the world, the love of the Father is not in him."

DIGGING DEEPER

1. Why do you want to please others?

2. In what ways do you tend to conform to the world?

3. What are some of the world's major influences on your life?

4. How have you tried to break away from worldly influences?

5. How do people "drink the cup of demons" in this age? How do you keep yourself free from their influence?

6. Why can't a people pleaser be a servant of Christ?

7. How have you been guilty of two-timing God?

8. When was a time that you put others' requests before God's requests?

9. What does "submit yourselves, then, to God" mean? Why is submission to God essential for the Christian?

10. What are some of the world's cultural values that really seem opposed to God's values?

11. How do you keep from being overpowered by the world's value structures?

12. How would you compare what the world has to give with what Jesus has to give?

13. How can you specifically "renew your mind" each day?

14. Since you have been a Christian, has the tug of the world been stronger or fainter?

COURAGE

JOAN OF ARC

In the first part of the 15th century, there lived a young French peasant by the name of Joan of Arc with her sacred sword, her consecrated banner, and her belief in her mission. While the fires were being lit around the stake on which this nineteen-year-old French peasant was to be burned alive, she was given a chance to regain her liberty by denying what she believed. Choosing fire above freedom, legend has her saying the following:

"Listen carefully. I know that not every man gives his life for what he believes nor every woman gives her life for what she believes. Sometimes people believe in little or nothing and yet they give their lives to that little or nothing. One life and we live it and thus it is gone, but to surrender what you are and live without belief is more terrible than dying young. But, there is a worse fate than dying without belief and that is to live with a firm commitment which at the end of life, at the portals of eternity, turns out to have betrayed you." Her last word as she died was a loud cry of "Jesus." While some of the English laughed, many people were brought to tears and some made professions of faith after hearing her words.

WHAT'S THE POINT?

Let me ask you a penetrating question. When you come to the end of your life and have nothing to look forward to except death and nothing to look back to except memories, what will it take to give you the confidence that you lived a life of significance and made an impact on your generation? When we think of courageous people, we tend to think of physical risk-takers, dare devils who jump out of planes, plunge off bridges, and generally love to put their lives in immediate peril. That's nerve. Real courage, however, is something deeper and it's usually a lot less showy. It's about standing up for your beliefs when a hundred voices shout you down. It's about saying "no" when friends dare you to take drugs or commit a crime and facing their mockery with pride. The cowardly lion thought that he needed the wizard to give him courage, but discovered he had it in him all along. Maybe your courage is tucked away inside waiting for just the right opportunity to come out.

MEDITATING ON GOD'S WORD

Joshua 10:25
"...Do not be afraid; do not be discouraged. Be strong and courageous."

2 Chronicles 19:11
"...Act with courage, and may the LORD be with those who do well."

Matthew 14:27
"...Take courage! It is I. Don't be afraid."

Matthew 13:21
"But since he has no root, he lasts only a short time. When trouble or persecution comes because of the word, he quickly falls away."

Acts 27:22
"But now I urge you to keep your courage..."

1 Corinthians 16:13
"Be on your guard; stand firm in the faith; be men of courage; be strong."

Hebrews 3:6
"...And we are his house, if we hold on to our courage and the hope of which we boast."

Revelation 3:16
"So, because you are lukewarm — neither hot or cold — I am about to spit you out of my mouth."

DIGGING DEEPER

1. What does courage mean to you? Is it possible to think of courage in a spiritual realm vs. a secular realm or do you think that the two go hand-in-hand?

2. Describe your life in one sentence in relation to courage. Why did you select that sentence?

3. What causes you to have a greater amount of courage?

4. How do you want to be remembered when you have passed away?

5. Would you have had the courage to say and do what Joan of Arc said and did?

6. If Jesus took your spiritual temperature today, what would he find? Why?

7. What's the most daring thing you have ever done?

8. What differences do you see between a difficult situation when your eyes are on Jesus and when they are on the difficult situation?

9. What was Jesus saying when he cried out "Take courage. It is I. Don't be afraid"?

A. Get yourselves together.

B. Don't panic.

C. Relax…Believe in me.

D. Why are you surprised…you saw me feed 5,000 people today.

10. What is some cargo you need to abandon in order to negotiate better through life's storms?

INJUSTICE

MARTIN NIEMÖLLER'S TESTIMONY

Following World War II, German Protestant leader Martin Niemöller on October 18, 1945 said, "The Nazis first came for the communists and I didn't speak up because I was not a communist. They came for the Jews and I did not speak up because I wasn't a Jew. Then they came for the trade unionists, and I didn't speak up because I wasn't a trade unionist. Then they came for the Catholics, but I didn't speak up because I was a Protestant. Then they came for me, and by that time there was no one to speak up for anyone."

WHAT'S THE POINT?

How do we deal with prejudice and hate? We shouldn't speak out against hate and injustice only because it is channeled towards us or it affects us! We should speak out because it is offensive, a crime against a fellow child of God.

MEDITATING ON GOD'S WORD

Exodus 22:21
"Do not mistreat an alien or oppress him."

1 Samuel 3:13
"For I told him that I would judge his family forever because of the sin he knew about; his sons made themselves contemptible and he [Eli, the High Priest] failed to restrain them."

Jeremiah 22:3

"This is what the LORD says: Do what is just and right. Rescue from the hand of his oppressor the one who has been robbed. Do no wrong or violence to the alien, the fatherless or the widow, and do not shed innocent blood in this place."

Luke 12:47

"The servant who knows his master's will and does not get ready or does not do what his master wants will be beaten with many blows."

John 12:43

"For they loved praise from men more than praise from God."

James 4:17

"Anyone, then, who knows the good he ought to do and doesn't do it, sins."

DIGGING DEEPER

1. Do you believe in "what goes around, comes around"? Why?

2. How can you help people whose experience is totally out of your realm of experience? What sometimes makes you feel uneasy about taking a stand for Christ?

3. Why do you think Niemöller didn't speak up?

4. Think of a time when you didn't speak up when an injustice to another was taking place and you could have gotten involved? What would you have done differently?

5. Respond to the following two quotes from people who, through faith, were able to respond to prejudice directed toward them or others in a positive way.

   Corrie Ten Boom: "Lord Jesus, I offer myself for Your people. In any way. Any place. Any time." (from: *The Hiding Place* by Corrie Ten Boom with John and Elizabeth Sherrill; Washington Depot, CT: Chosen Books, 1971; page 73).

Martin Luther King: "An individual has not started living until he can rise above the narrow confines of his individualistic concerns to the broader concerns of all humanity." (from: "The Words of Martin Luther King, Jr.", selected by Coretta Scott King; New York: Newmarket Press, 1983).

6. Who was Niemöller most like in the story of the Good Samaritan found in Luke 10:25-37? What do you think you would have done if you saw someone hurt on the side of the road? What if it was someone at your school who was not of the same race, social class, religion, political persuasion, or clique as you?

30

PURPOSE

MAKE ME A FORK IN THE ROAD

Jim Elliot gave his life to the Auca tribe, as many of us know. The beautiful little book, *Through Gates of Splendor*, tells how he, along with several others, landed a little missionary plane in Central America and they were all harpooned to death.

When did it all begin for Jim Elliot? It began in college in Wheaton when God really did speak to him about his own commitment to Christ. Jim Elliot wrote one day, "Lord, make me a fork in the road so that when people meet me they have got to decide about you. Make me a fork in the road."

WHAT'S THE POINT?

When you reach a fork in the road, there are only two ways to go: either to the left or the right. When you commit to the Lord, you need to be *hot*. The Bible says that if you are lukewarm, you will be spit out (Revelation 3:15-16). You either serve the Lord or the Devil; there is no in between. Jesus' last request was to "go and make disciples." There are no bystander Christians. We are all called to march in the army of the King. Many may suffer. Many may turn around and go back. This should not slow us down.

MEDITATING ON GOD'S WORD

Psalm 23:3
"He guides me in paths of righteousness for his name's sake."

Psalm 119:105
"Your word is a lamp to my feet and a light for my path."

Proverbs 4:25
"Let your eyes look straight ahead, fix your gaze directly before you."

Matthew 7:13-14
"Enter through the narrow gate. For wide is the gate and broad is the road that leads to destruction, and many enter through it. But small is the gate and narrow the road that leads to life, and only a few find it."

Matthew 28:19
"Therefore, go and make disciples of all nations, baptizing them in the name of the Father and of the Son and of the Holy Spirit."

Luke 14:23
"A certain man was preparing a great banquet and invited many guests...Then the master told his servant, 'Go out to the roads and country lanes and make them come in, so that my house will be full.'"

Acts 1:8
"But you will receive power when the Holy Spirit comes on you; and you will be my witnesses in Jerusalem, and in all Judea and Samaria, and to the ends of the earth."

2 Timothy 4:9-10
"Do your best to come to me quickly, for Demas, because he loved this world, has deserted me and has gone to Thessalonica."

Hebrews 12:12-13
"Therefore, strengthen your feeble arms and weak knees. Make level paths for your feet, so that the lame may not be disabled, but rather healed."

DIGGING DEEPER

1. What are the ways that you serve the Lord?

2. Have there been times in your life when you have felt that you took the wrong road? Describe the road. How did you get back on the right road?

3. What are ways that you can influence people on your school campus to make a decision about Christ?

4. What are things that hold you back from sharing your faith with somebody?

5. Who are three friends you can pray for concerning a decision for Christ?

6. What is one of the biggest challenges you have ever faced? How successfully did you face it? What resources helped?

7. What central command did Jesus leave his disciples? How are they to carry it out?

8. What do you see as your responsibility in carrying out the great commission?

9. What excuses have you heard from non-Christians about why they don't want to come to the banquet?

10. What keeps people out of the kingdom?

11. What is your "Jerusalem, Judea, Samaria..."?

12. Have you seen Christian friends who have loved the world more than the Lord? How have they affected your spiritual journey? What can you do to reach them?

31

CREATED AND BOUGHT

BOAT IN THE WINDOW

A young boy spent many hours building a little sailboat, crafting it down to the finest detail. He then took it to a nearby river to sail it. When he put it in the water, however, it moved away from him very quickly. Though he chased it along the bank, he couldn't keep up with it. The strong wind and current carried the boat away. The heartbroken boy knew how hard he would have to work to build another sailboat.

Farther down the river, a man found the little boat, took it to town, and sold it to a shopkeeper. Later that day, as the boy was walking through town, he noticed the boat in a store window.

Entering the store, he told the owner that the boat belonged to him. It had his own little marks on it, but he couldn't prove to the shopkeeper that the boat was his. The man told him the only way he could get the boat was to buy it. The boy wanted it back so badly that he did exactly that.

As he took the boat from the hand of the shopkeeper, he looked at it and said, "Little boat, you're twice mine. I made you and I bought you."

WHAT'S THE POINT?

In the same way, we are twice God's. Our Father in heaven both created us and paid a great price for us. With the blood of his Son, we have been redeemed and reunited with God.

Jesus Christ gave his life to get us back, yet so often we show such little gratitude for what he has done for us.

MEDITATING ON GOD'S WORD

Genesis 1:27
"So God created man in his own image, in the image of God he created him; male and female he created them."

Psalm 139:13-14
"For you created my inmost being; you knit me together in my mother's womb. I praise you because I am fearfully and wonderfully made; your works are wonderful, I know that full well."

Ecclesiastes 12:1
"Remember your Creator in the days of your youth..."

John 15:13
"Greater love has no one than this, that he lay down his life for his friends."

Romans 5:8
"But God demonstrates his own love for us in this: While we were still sinners, Christ died for us."

1 Corinthians 6:19-20
"...You are not your own: you were bought at a price..."

Colossians 1:16
"For by him all things were created: things in heaven and on earth, visible and invisible, whether thrones or powers or rulers or authorities; all things were created by him and for him."

Revelation 4:11
"You are worthy, our Lord and God, to receive glory and honor and power, for you created all things and by your will they were created and have their being."

DIGGING DEEPER

1. If these verses are true, what position should Jesus have in your life? Why?

2. In what area of your life do you have the most difficulty giving Christ supremacy? Why? What will you do today to begin eliminating this difficulty?

3. How can you give God glory and honor and power in your own life today?

4. How does it feel to know Jesus made you and then paid for you with his life? What do you want to say to Jesus?

5. When you read that God created you, did you want to thank him or complain to him? Why? How do you think God feels about your response to his creation (meaning you)?

LETTING GO

BEGGAR'S RAGS

A beggar lived near the king's palace. One day he saw a proclamation posted outside the palace gate. The king was giving a great dinner. Anyone dressed in royal garments was invited to the party.

The beggar went on his way. He looked at the rags he was wearing and sighed. Surely only kings and their families wore royal robes, he thought.

Slowly an idea crept into his mind. The audacity of it made him tremble. Would he dare?

He made his way back to the palace. He approached the guard at the gate. "Please, sire, I would like to speak to the king."

"Wait here," the guard replied.

In a few minutes he was back. "His majesty will see you," he said, and led the beggar in.

"You wished to see me?" asked the king.

"Yes, your majesty. I want so much to attend the banquet, but I have no royal robes to wear. Please, sir, if I may be so bold, may I have one of your old garments so that I, too, may come to the banquet?"

The beggar shook so hard that he could not see the faint smile that was on the king's face.

"You have been wise in coming to me," the king said. He called to his son, the young prince. "Take this man to your room and array him in some of your clothes."

The prince did as he was told and soon the beggar was standing before a mirror, clothed in garments that he had never dared hope for.

"You are now eligible to attend the king's banquet tomorrow night," said the prince. "But even more important, you will never need any other clothes. These garments will last forever."

The beggar dropped to his knees. "Oh, thank you," he cried. But as he started to leave, he looked back at his pile of dirty rags on the floor. He hesitated. What if the prince was wrong? What if he would need his old clothes again? Quickly he gathered them up.

The banquet was far greater than he had ever imagined, but he could not enjoy himself as he should. He had made a small bundle of his old rags and it kept falling off his lap. The food was passed quickly and the beggar missed some of the greatest delicacies.

Time proved that the prince was right. The clothes lasted forever. Still the poor beggar grew fonder and fonder of his old rags.

As time passed, people seemed to forget the royal robes he was wearing. They saw only the little bundle of filthy rags that he clung to wherever he went. They even spoke of him as the old man with the rags.

One day as he lay dying, the king visited him. The beggar saw the sad look on the king's face when he looked at the small bundle of rags by the bed. Suddenly the beggar remembered the prince's words and he realized that his bundle of rags had cost him a lifetime of true royalty. He wept bitterly at his folly and the king wept with him.

(From *More Hot Illustrations for Youth,* by Wayne Rice. Copyright 1995 by Youth Specialties. Used by permission.)

WHAT'S THE POINT?

We have been invited into a royal family — the family of God. To feast at God's dinner table, all we have to do is shed our old rags and put on the "new clothes" of faith which is provided by God's Son, Jesus Christ.

But we cannot hold onto our old rags. When we put our faith in Christ, we must let go of the sin in our life and our old ways of living. Those things must be discarded if we are to experience true royalty and abundant life in Christ. "Behold, the old is passed away; the new has come!"

MEDITATING ON GOD'S WORD

Isaiah 64:6
"All of us have become like one who is unclean, and all our righteous acts are like filthy rags."

2 Corinthians 5:17
"Therefore, if anyone is in Christ, he is a new creation; the old has gone, the new has come!"

Ephesians 6:10-17
"Finally, be strong in the Lord and in his mighty power. Put on the full armor of God so that you can take your stand against the devil's schemes. For our struggle is not against flesh and blood, but against the rulers, against the authorities, against the powers of this dark world, and against the spiritual forces of evil in the heavenly realms. Therefore put on the full armor of God, so that when the day of evil comes, you may be able to stand your ground, and after you have done everything, to stand. Stand firm then, with the belt of truth buckled around your waist, with the breastplate of righteousness in place, and with your feet fitted with the readiness that comes from the gospel of peace. In addition to all this, take up the shield of faith, with which you can extinguish all the flaming arrows of the evil one. Take the helmet of salvation and the sword of the Spirit, which is the word of God."

Revelation 21:5
"He who was seated on the throne said, 'I am making everything new!'"

DIGGING DEEPER

1. What piece of spiritual armor do you need most at this point in your life? Are you wearing it?

2. What evidence do you have in your life that you are a new creation?

3. Has there been a time in your life when you "went back to your old rags"? How did that make you feel? What did you do about it?

4. How does it make you feel when you read that you are a member of a royal family?

5. What is different about your life since you became a Christian?

6. How can you guard against picking up the old rags in your life, the rags that cause you to miss out on enjoying true royalty?

33

POSSIBILITIES

JESSE OWENS' STORY

In his book *The Heart of a Champion*, Bob Richards tells the story of Olympic champion Charley Paddock, who was a great speaker and loved to talk to young people in high school. Once, while speaking at East Tech High School in Cleveland, Ohio, he challenged, "If you think you can, you can. If you believe a thing strongly enough, it can come to pass in your life!"

Afterward, he lifted his hand and said, "Who knows but there's an Olympic champion here in this auditorium this afternoon!" Later, a spindly-legged black young person said to Mr. Paddock, "Mr. Paddock, I'd give anything if I could be an Olympic champion just like you!" It was that lad's moment of inspiration. From that moment on, his life was changed. In 1936, that young man went to Berlin, Germany and won four gold medals. His name was Jesse Owens. Back home, he was driven through the streets of Cleveland to the cheers of the crowd. The car stopped and he signed some autographs. A little skinny black child pressing against the car said, "Mr. Owens, I'd give anything if I could be an Olympic champion just like you." Jesse reached out to this little fellow, who was nicknamed "Bones," and said, "You know, young fellow, that's what I wanted to be when I was a little older than you are. If you'll work and train and believe, then you can become an Olympic champion."

Well, that little fellow was so inspired he ran all the way home. Bob Richards writes, "That little fellow told me that when he got home, he ran up to his grandmother and said, "Grandma, I'm going to become an Olympic champion!" At Wembley Stadium in London, England in 1948, six boys waited for the gun to go off for the finals of the 100-meter dash. The gun cracked. The young man in the outside lane burst out, drove down to hit the tape, and won. His name: Harrison "Bones" Dillard. He tied Jesse Owens' Olympic record and went on to break more world records.

WHAT'S THE POINT?

"You say it's fantastic?" Richards asks. "You're saying that it'll never happen again? And I tell you you're wrong. It'll happen again and again, in young men and women who are inspired. Who will catch a vision of what they can become, who will see not skinny legs or spindly legs, but who will catch a vision of Olympic champions." They will rise through training and perseverance and hard work and they will be champions. As Jesse Owens followed Charley Paddock and Harrison "Bones" Dillard followed Jesse Owens to become Olympic champions, we are to follow Jesus. Jesus offers no great promises of power, popularity, prestige, or riches. He does call us to a life of excitement and challenges. With Jesus empowering you, all things are possible.

MEDITATING ON GOD'S WORD

Matthew 14:28
"'Lord, if it's you,' Peter replied, 'tell me to come to you on the water.' 'Come,' he said."

Matthew 17:20
"...I tell you the truth, if you have faith as small as a mustard seed, you can say to this mountain, 'Move from here to there' and it will move. Nothing will be impossible for you."

Matthew 19:26
"...With man this is impossible, but with God all things are possible."

Mark 9:23
"...Everything is possible for him who believes."

Mark 10:27
"…With man this is impossible, but not with God; all things are possible with God."

Mark 14:36
"Abba, Father…everything is possible for you."

Luke 1:37
"For nothing is impossible with God."

Luke 18:27
"…What is impossible with men is possible with God."

John 12:26
"Whoever serves me must follow me."

DIGGING DEEPER

1. Are you willing to follow Jesus even if it means ridicule, having people turn their back on you, and sacrifice?

2. What's the most daring thing you have ever done? What made it so daring?

3. In Matthew 14, Peter gets out of the boat and walks on the water with Jesus. Would you have been more likely to stay in the boat or step out of it? Why?

4. When faced with a difficult situation, what effect does keeping your eyes on Jesus instead of the waves have on your decisions?

5. In what area do you feel God is inviting you to "get out of the boat" right now?

6. If you could move a mountain, which mountain would you move first? Why?

7. What does Jesus mean when he says "Everything is possible for him who believes"? Where does prayer fit into belief?

8. In what area of your life do you need to believe that "nothing is impossible with God"? What keeps you from believing this? Do you need to claim this problem today?

34

GOD'S FORGIVENESS

RUNAWAY FROM MILPITAS

The gospel is like a young girl in Milpitas, California. She had normal parents, but they just got on her nerves. They didn't like it when she pierced her body. They didn't like the clothes she wore. They didn't like the music she listened to. She was sick of it. One day she wrote them a note and took off. She ended up in Casper, Wyoming. When she was there, she met a man who was nicer to her than any man she had ever met before. He drove the biggest car she had ever seen. He gave her pills that made her feel better than she had ever felt before and things were pretty nice for a year. But then she got sick. The man took advantage of her sexually and suddenly no one wanted her anymore. This guy she called boss who had been so nice to her suddenly kicked her out of the place she was staying and he wouldn't have anything to do with her.

It gets pretty cold in Casper, Wyoming. One night, she was huddled up over a heating grate outside a department store pulling old newspapers, cardboard boxes, and an old coat over her trying to stay warm and trying to sleep. A fourteen-year-old girl doesn't get much sleep outdoors in the city. It was almost as if she were hallucinating as she thought of her Irish Setter back in Milpitas romping around chasing butterflies in the backyard. It suddenly struck her, stabbing her in the heart as she thought about how her dog had it better. He was eating better and was being treated better than she was.

She called her folks, got an answering machine, and left a message. She told her folks that she was taking a bus and told them the specific time when she would arrive in two days. She said "You may not even know that I am still alive, but if you still want to see me, I will get off the bus. If you don't, I guess I will stay on it and maybe go to Canada. She got on the bus and as she drove that long way through the snow-swept plains, she realized what a stupid plan it was. What if her parents were away for the weekend? What if they never got the message? Her whole life was being decided.

Finally, the bus pulled in. The driver made an announcement over the crackling microphone, "Fifteen minutes folks, that's all we have fifteen minutes." Fifteen minutes she had to decide her life. All the way back, she had rehearsed an apology: "I'm sorry, Dad. It was all my fault. You were not so bad. I'm sorry; it was all my fault." She walked in the concrete block terminal. She had thought through a thousand different things but she hadn't thought through what actually happened. Her dad was there; her mother was there; her sister was there; her two brothers were there; her aunt was there; her uncle was there; her great aunt, grandmother, and grandfather were there. There were 200 people crammed into that waiting room. Across the back of that terminal was a computer-generated banner that said "Welcome home, welcome home."

(Adapted from a message given by Philip Yancey at the Youth Specialties National Convention in 1996.)

WHAT'S THE POINT?

In Jesus' version of the story, found in Luke 15:11-27 the prodigal son had no time to give his well-rehearsed story. This is a story of God's incredible, undeserving love and mercy that he extends to us. God not only loves us; he likes us and is delighted when we return home to him.

MEDITATING ON GOD'S WORD

Deuteronomy 4:31
"For the LORD your God is a merciful God; he will not abandon or destroy you."

Numbers 14:18
"The LORD is slow to anger, abounding in love and forgiving sin and rebellion."

Psalm 78:38
"Yet he was merciful; he forgave their iniquities and did not destroy them. Time after time he restrained his anger and did not stir up his full wrath."

Psalm 86:5
"You are forgiving and good, O Lord, abounding in love to all who call to you."

Psalm 103:12
"As far as the east is from the west, so far has he removed our transgressions from us."

Psalm 145:8
"The LORD is gracious and compassionate, slow to anger and rich in love."

Lamentations 3:25
"The LORD is good to those whose hope is in him, to the one who seeks him."

Nahum 1:7
"The LORD is good, a refuge in times of trouble."

Luke 15:4-7
"Suppose one of you has a hundred sheep and loses one of them. Does he not leave the ninety-nine in the open country and go after the lost sheep until he finds it? And when he finds it, he joyfully puts it on his shoulders and goes home. Then he calls his friends together and says, 'Rejoice with me; I have found my lost sheep.' I tell you that in the same way there will be more rejoicing in heaven over one sinner who repents than over ninety-nine righteous persons who do not need to repent."

Romans 5:8
"But God demonstrated his own love for us in this: while we were still sinners, Christ died for us."

1 John 1:9
"If we confess our sins, he is faithful and just and will forgive us our sins and purify us from all unrighteousness."

DIGGING DEEPER

1. What have been your stages in your spiritual pilgrimage?

2. When you know you have sinned, how long does it take you to confess? Why?

3. What is your part and what is God's part in the confession process?

4. If you spent more time praising God and less time thinking about problems, what would happen? Why?

5. Have you ever been a lost son/daughter? How did Jesus find you and bring you back?

6. Why do you think God cares this much for one sinner? What does this say about our relationship with God?

7. What stages did the prodigal son/daughter go through? What brought him/her to his/her senses?

8. What do you think the father was doing while his son/daughter was away?

9. If you had to compare your spiritual journey to the prodigal's journey, where are you now?

10. What is the lesson for you in this parable?

PRAYER JOURNAL
CONCERNS/REQUESTS

DATE	CONCERN/REQUEST	DATE	ANSWER

PRAYER JOURNAL
CONCERNS/REQUESTS

DATE	CONCERN/REQUEST	DATE	ANSWER

PRAYER JOURNAL
PRAISES

DATE	PRAISE

PRAYER JOURNAL
PRAISES

DATE	PRAISE

ABOUT THE AUTHOR

Les Christie was born in Liverpool, England and at age five moved to California with his family. He graduated from Pacific Christian College and Iuller Sheological eminary. He is the chairman of the youth ministry department at San Jose Christian College.

Les has been in youth ministry for thirty years. He was youth minister at Eastside Christian Church in Fullerton, California for twenty-two years. Les has spoken to more than two million high school students and trained hundreds of thousands of adult youth workers in forty-two states and ten foreign countries. He is the author of nine books and the co-author of an additional nine books.

Les and his wife Gretchen live in San Jose, California with their two teenage sons, Brent and David. If you want to get ahold of Les he can be reached by writing or calling:

Les Christie
San Jose Christian College
P.O. Box 1090
San Jose, CA 95108
(408) 293-9058

Notes

Notes

Notes

Notes

Notes

Notes

Notes

Notes

Notes

Notes